Sound Projects

with a

MUSIC LAB

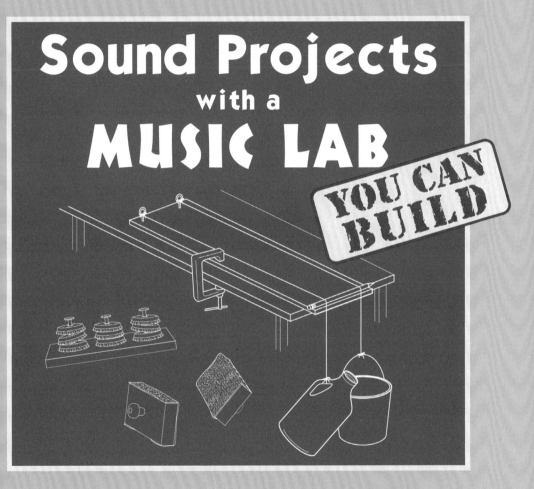

YOU CAN BUILD

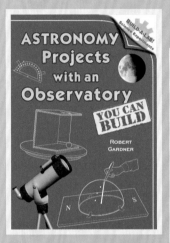

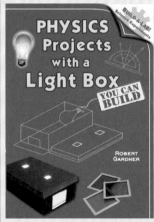

BUILD-A-LAB!
SCIENCE EXPERIMENTS

Sound Projects
with a
MUSIC LAB

YOU CAN BUILD

ROBERT GARDNER

Enslow Publishers, Inc.
40 Industrial Road
Box 398
Berkeley Heights, NJ 07922
USA

http://www.enslow.com

Copyright © 2008 by Robert Gardner

Library of Congress Cataloging-in-Publication Data:

Gardner, Robert, 1929–
    Sound projects with a music lab you can build / by Robert Gardner.
      p. cm. — (Build-a-lab! Science experiments)
    Summary: "Introduces information on sound through a variety of related experiments using a musical lab that the reader can build"—Provided by publisher.
    Includes bibliographical references and index.
    ISBN-13: 978-0-7660-2809-8
    ISBN-10: 0-7660-2809-7
    1. Sound—Juvenile literature. 2. Sound—Experiments—Juvenile literature.
3. Science projects—Juvenile literature. I. Title.
    QC225.5.G376 2008
    534.078—dc22

                                 2007019458

Printed in the United States of America

10 9 8 7 6 5 4 3 2 1

Illustration credits: Jonathan Moreno

Photo credits: Enslow Publishers, Inc.

Cover photo: Enslow Publishers, Inc.

CONTENTS

⚙

INTRODUCTION 7

Science Fairs. 9

The Scientific Method 11

Safety 12

CH. 1   THE SCIENCE OF SOUND 14

🏅1-1   Vibrations: The Cause of Sounds 15

1-2   A Bull Roarer. 21

1-3   Sound, Frequency, and Pitch 22

🏅1-4   How Sound Travels. 24

1-5   A Sound Trumpet 31

🏅1-6   Sound in Solids and Liquids 32

CH. 2   SCIENCE AND MUSIC 36

2-1   The Science of Strings 37

2-2   Waves, Standing Waves, and Harmonics 41

🏅2-3   Waves, Octaves, Music, and Math 45

🏅2-4   A String Telephone and a "Bell" 48

🏅2-5   A Vibrating Air Column 51

🏅2-6   Resonance 54

🏅2-7   Sounds of the Sea: Resonance with
Tubes of Air. 59

CH. 3   INSTRUMENTS WITH STRINGS 60

🏅3-1   What Is the Purpose of a Mute on
a Stringed Instrument? 62

3-2   Why Is There a Hollow Box Under the Strings? 64

3-3   A Wide-Keyed "Piano" 65

🏅3-4   A Twangy "Piano" 67

EXPERIMENTS WITH A 🏅 SYMBOL FEATURE IDEAS FOR YOUR SCIENCE FAIR.

CONTENTS

3-5   A One-String Guitar 69
3-6   A Two-String Bottle Banjo 73
3-7   An Eight-String Harp 78
3-8   A "Washtub" Bass 81
3-9   A Shoe Box Guitar 85

Ch. 4 WIND INSTRUMENTS 87
4-1   A Hose Horn 88
4-2   A Simple Pipe Organ 89
4-3   A Fluty Horn 92
4-4   A Bottle Band 94
4-5   A Panpipe 96
4-6   Reed Horns 100

Ch. 5 PERCUSSION INSTRUMENTS 104
5-1   A Mechanic's Xylophone 106
5-2   Drinking Glass Bells 107
5-3   The Bell and Woodwind Mystery 109
5-4   A Mechanic's Chimes 110
5-5   Bells from Flowerpots 112
5-6   Wood Chimes and Other Chimes 114
5-7   Some Inexpensive Percussion Instruments 117
      Appendix: Science Supply Companies 121
      Further Reading 124
      Internet Addresses 125
      Index 126

EXPERIMENTS WITH A 🎗 SYMBOL FEATURE IDEAS FOR YOUR SCIENCE FAIR.

INTRODUCTION

Stop! Listen! How many different sounds can you hear? Do you hear horns, music, voices, telephones, engines, electronic humming?

Nature is full of music and rhythm—the songs that birds and whales sing, the hoofbeats of a galloping horse, waves breaking on a beach, a babbling brook, rumbling thunder, wind whistling through trees, croaking frogs, and chirping crickets.

There are noises—and there is music. People can both speak and sing. The sounds of speech and music come from our vocal cords, but they are very different.

Some anthropologists believe that our human ancestors hummed, danced, and played music before they talked. We know for certain that early humans made music because flutes made of bird bones have been found at sites known to be at least 36,000 years old. We know, too, that the early ancestors of humans, a species known as *Australopithecus afarensis*, were walking on two feet at least 3 million years ago. Were they dancing to the rhythm of beating drums?

We don't know, but music, dance, and rhythm are so much a part of human behavior that it seems likely.

In this book, you will learn how to build a variety of different simple musical instruments. You will also do a number of experiments related to sound and music. The experiments will provide a basis for understanding the science that applies to musical instruments.

Unlike other books in this *Build-a-Lab* series, we will not begin by building something. Instead, we will start by learning some of the science needed to understand how musical instruments work.

Many of the things required to build the instruments and do the experiments can be found in your home. You may have to shop for some of the others. You can find them in a supermarket; a sports, hobby, or toy shop; a hardware store; a plant nursery; or one of the science supply houses listed in the appendix.

At times, you may need one or more people to help you. It would be best if you work with friends or adults who enjoy experimenting as much as you do. In that way, you will all enjoy what you are doing. **If any danger is involved in doing** an experiment, it will be made known to you. In some cases, to avoid any danger, you will be asked to work with an adult. Please do so. We don't want you to take any chances that could lead to an injury.

Like any good scientist, you will find it useful to record ideas, notes, data, and anything you can conclude from your experiments in a notebook. As you do this, you can keep track of the information you gather and the conclusions you reach. The notebook will allow you to refer to experiments you have done in the past and help you in doing future projects.

SCIENCE FAIRS

Some of the experiments in this book contain ideas you might use for a science fair. Those projects are indicated with a 🏵 symbol. However, judges at science fairs do not reward projects or experiments that are simply copied from a book. For example, a diagram of a sound wave would not impress most judges. Instead, an experiment that shows the mathematical relationship of tension, length, and thickness of a wire to the frequency at which it vibrates would be more likely to attract their attention.

Science fair judges tend to reward creative thought and imagination. It is difficult to be creative or imaginative unless you are really interested in your project; therefore, try to choose an investigation that appeals to you. And before you jump into a project, consider, too, your own talents and the cost of the materials you will need.

If you decide to use an experiment or idea found in this book for a science fair, you should find ways to modify or extend it. This should not be difficult because you will discover that as you do experiments, new ideas will come to mind. You will think of experiments that could make excellent science fair projects, particularly because the ideas are your own and are interesting to you.

If you have never prepared for a science fair, you should read some of the books listed in the Further Reading section. These books deal specifically with science fairs. They provide plenty of helpful hints and useful information that will help you to avoid the pitfalls that sometimes plague first-time entrants. You will learn how to prepare appealing reports that include charts and graphs, how to set up and display your work, how to present your project, and how to relate to judges and visitors.

THE SCIENTIFIC METHOD

Doing a science fair project, particularly one that involves original research, will require you to use what is commonly called the scientific method. In many science textbooks you will find a section devoted to the subject. It will probably tell you that the scientific method consists of a series of steps. However, many scientists do not follow a set pattern that leads them to new knowledge. Each investigation is unique and requires different techniques, procedures, and thought processes. Perhaps the best description of the scientific method was given by Nobel Prize-winning physicist Percy Bridgman. He said that the scientific method is doing one's best with one's mind, no holds barred.

The idea that there is a set scientific method that all scientists follow probably came about because of the way scientists report their findings. These reports are very similar in format and include the problem or question, the hypothesis (what you think will happen), the experimental procedure that tests the hypothesis, the results, and a conclusion. You will follow a similar format if you prepare a report on a science fair project. The format will include searching references like science publications, coming up with a question, and forming a hypothesis. You will then explain how your experiment was done and report your results. You will need to describe any relationships or patterns in the experimental variables and controls that may lead your conclusion.

SAFETY

Most of the projects included in this book are perfectly safe. However, the following safety rules are well worth reading before you start any project.

1. Do any experiments or projects, whether from this book or of your own design, **under the supervision of a science teacher or other knowledgeable adult.**

2. Read all instructions carefully before proceeding with a project. If you have questions, check with your supervisor before going any further.

3. Maintain a serious attitude while conducting experiments. Fooling around can be dangerous to you and to others.

4. **Always wear safety goggles** if there is any possibility of something, such as a nail or rubber band, striking your eye.

5. Do not eat or drink while experimenting.

6. Have a first aid kit nearby while you are experimenting.

7. Never experiment with household electricity. Instead, use batteries.

8. **Wash your hands** thoroughly after completing an experiment.

THE SCIENCE OF SOUND

Before you build your own musical instruments, it will be useful to understand the science of sound and music. In this chapter you will investigate the science of sound. In Chapter 2 you will explore the science related to musical sounds. An understanding of the science behind sound and music will give you a better understanding of how musical instruments work. As you will see, musical sounds involve frequency. Frequency is the number of times something is repeated in a certain period of time. The unit used for frequency in science is the hertz (Hz). Something that happens once per second has a frequency of 1 Hz. The unit is named in honor of Heinrich Rudolf Hertz (1857–1894), whose experiments led to the development of radio.

As you will see in the first experiment, sounds, including musical notes, are caused by vibrations. Vibrations are any regularly repeated to-and-fro motion or change, such as a plucked banjo string, a swinging pendulum, or an insect's flapping wings. Can you think of other vibrating things?

1. **Hang a thin rubber band** over a doorknob. Stretch the rubber band with one hand. Then pluck the stretched rubber band with a finger. You will hear a sound. What is happening to the rubber band while it makes a sound?

2. Hold one end of a stiff 1-ft (30-cm) ruler firmly against the edge of a tabletop as shown in Figure 1. Pluck the other end with your finger. What do you notice about the ruler while it is making a sound?

You Will Need

- thin rubber band
- doorknob
- stiff 1-ft (30-cm) ruler
- table
- yardstick or meterstick
- large balloon
- wineglasses
- waxed paper
- comb
- kazoo
- plastic wrap
- empty cylindrical oatmeal box
- salt
- cooking pot
- spoon
- tape
- thread
- Ping-Pong ball
- tuning fork and mallet
- drinking glass
- water

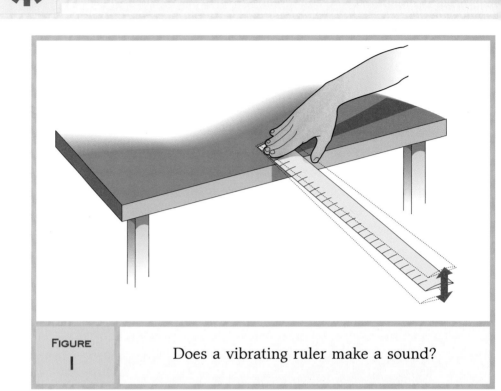

FIGURE
1

Does a vibrating ruler make a sound?

A sound's pitch is the sensation that it produces in a listener. A high pitch, such as notes sung by a soprano, result from vibrations that have a high frequency. A low pitch, such as notes sung by a bass voice, are the result of low-frequency vibrations.

3. Shorten the length of the ruler that extends beyond the table, then pluck it again. Is the pitch made by the ruler higher or lower than it was before? What has happened to the frequency with which it vibrates?

4. Now lengthen the part of the ruler that extends beyond

the table and pluck it again. What happens to the pitch of the sound made by the ruler? What has happened to the frequency at which it vibrates?

5. Repeat this experiment with a yardstick or meterstick. You may not hear a sound when most of the stick extends beyond the table. The reason is that human ears cannot detect sounds with frequencies less than 20 Hz. The highest frequency that humans can hear is about 20,000 Hz. That range of hearing often decreases with age. Dogs have better hearing. Their range extends from 15 to 50,000 Hz. You may have a dog whistle that your dog can hear even though you can't. Dolphins have an even wider range of hearing. Their range extends from 150 to 150,000 Hz.

6. Hold the fingers of one hand on your throat as you sing a note. Can you feel the vibrations of the vocal cords inside your larynx (Adam's apple)?

7. Fill a large balloon with air and seal its neck. Hold the balloon in front of your mouth, using the fingertips of both hands. Speak some words. Can you feel the skin of the balloon vibrating?

8. Sing, or have a friend sing, a high note (high pitch) at the balloon. Then sing a low note (low pitch). Can you feel a difference in the frequency at which the skin of the balloon vibrates?

9. With one hand, hold the base of a wineglass on a table. Wet the index finger of your other hand and move it gently around the rim of the wineglass. You will hear a high-pitched ringing sound.

10. Add water to the glass. Does the addition of water affect the pitch of the sound you hear? If it does, does it make the pitch higher or lower?

11. Try this experiment with wineglasses of different sizes. Does the size of the glass affect the sound? If it does, how is the sound's pitch related to the size of the glass?

12. Wrap a piece of waxed paper loosely around a comb. Place the comb between your lips and hum. Can you feel the paper vibrating? What kind of sound do you hear? Does it sound similar to a kazoo, which you can buy in a party store? How do you think a kazoo produces its sound?

13. Stretch a piece of plastic wrap over the open end of an empty oatmeal box. Use a rubber band to keep it tightly stretched.

Sprinkle some table salt on the plastic. Hold a cooking pot upside down over the plastic, but not touching it. Hit the bottom of the pot with a spoon. What happens to the salt grains?

How do the salt grains react to other sounds such as your voice when you speak or sing? What do you think causes the salt grains to behave as they do?

14. Tape a thread to a Ping-Pong ball. Strike a tine of a tuning fork by tapping it with the soft-headed mallet that comes with a tuning fork. Or tap the tuning fork against the rubber heel of your shoe. Then bring the suspended ball near a tine of the vibrating tuning fork. What happens to the ball? Can you explain why it happens?

15. Predict what will happen if you strike a tuning fork tine and then lower the tines into a glass of water. Was your prediction correct? How can you explain what you observe?

IDEA FOR YOUR SCIENCE FAIR

How can people measure the range of sound frequencies that animals can hear?

ULTRASOUND AND INFRASOUND

Sounds with frequencies greater than 20,000 Hz cannot be heard by humans. Such high-pitched sounds are called ultrasound. Ultrasound is used extensively in medicine. Machines that produce ultrasound beam these sounds into parts of the human body. The reflected sounds are used to create images. For example, ultrasound is used to examine a fetus within a mother's womb.

Sonar, short for *so*und *na*vigation *r*anging, operates by sending ultrasound down into the ocean. By measuring the time for the reflected sounds to return, the depth of the ocean at that point can be determined.

Sounds with frequencies less than 20 Hz (infrasound) cannot be heard by humans either. Such sounds can, however, cause parts of your body to vibrate and damage body tissues.

Elephants are believed to communicate with one another using infrasound. These low pitched sounds, made in the throat of an elephant, can be heard miles away by other members of the herd.

A BULL ROARER

I n this experiment you will see how sounds can be created by making the air vibrate.

1. Find a thin piece of wood about 12 in (30 cm) long, 1 in (2.5 cm) wide, and 1/4 in (0.5 cm) thick. **Ask an adult** to drill a small hole near one end of the stick. Thread one end of a 3-ft– (90-cm–) long piece of twine through the hole. Tie that end of the twine securely to the stick.

2. Take the stick outside to an open area away from people and buildings. Hold the free end of the twine in your hand. Swing the stick above your head. Describe the sound you hear.

3. Do the experiment again using a wider piece of wood. How does the sound produced by swinging the larger stick compare with the sound you heard when you swung the smaller stick? Can you explain any difference in the sounds made by the two sticks?

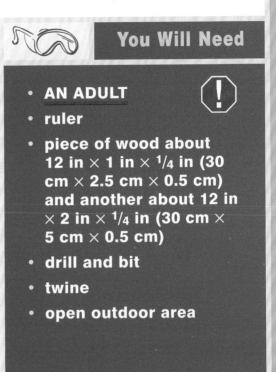

You Will Need

- **AN ADULT**
- **ruler**
- **piece of wood about 12 in × 1 in × 1/4 in (30 cm × 2.5 cm × 0.5 cm) and another about 12 in × 2 in × 1/4 in (30 cm × 5 cm × 0.5 cm)**
- **drill and bit**
- **twine**
- **open outdoor area**

SOUND, FREQUENCY AND PITCH

1. **Turn a bicycle upside down** so that the seat and handlebars are resting on the ground. Use a clothespin to attach a 3-in × 5-in index card to the frame of the bicycle. Attach the card in such a way that its corner will touch the spokes of the back wheel when the wheel turns.

2. Use your hand to turn the pedals so that the wheel begins to turn. Turn slowly at first. As long as the card hits the spokes less than 20 times per second, you will hear a tapping sound.

When you turn the wheel faster, so that the card collides with the spokes more than 20 times per second, you may hear a low-pitched sound. Continue increasing the wheel's speed. You will hear the pitch become higher because the frequency with which card and spokes are colliding is increasing.

You Will Need

- **bicycle**
- **clothespin**
- **3-in × 5-in index card**
- **tuning forks—256, 288, and 512 Hz**
- **soft-headed mallet or rubber-soled shoe**

   (You might borrow tuning forks and a mallet from a science or music teacher.)

You can probably hear sounds between 20 and 20,000 Hz. A sound with a constant pitch can be made with an electronic oscillator or with a tuning fork. A common tuning fork is one that vibrates at 256 Hz (middle C). A piano is tuned slightly different. Middle C on a piano is 261.6 Hz.

3. Strike such a tuning fork with a soft-headed mallet. Or strike the tuning fork against the rubber heel of your shoe. Then hold the tines of the fork near your ear. Now do the same with a tuning fork that has a different frequency. One with a frequency of 512 Hz will vibrate twice as fast as the one at 256 Hz. Can you detect its higher pitch? Listen to a tuning fork with a frequency of 256 Hz and one with a slightly higher frequency such as 288 Hz. Can you detect the difference in pitch? Some people who are tone deaf cannot.

HOW SOUND TRAVELS

As you have found, a sound is made when something vibrates. You have also found that sound can travel through air. In fact, most of the sounds we hear reach our ears by traveling through air. Sound moves away from its source as waves. In air at 68°F (20°C), sound waves travel at a speed of about 762 mph (1,235 $^{km}/_{hr}$) or about 1,125 $^{ft}/_s$ (343 $^m/_s$).

The vibrating string of a guitar, for example, pushes against air, creating a series of waves that travel through the air to your ears. Your vibrating vocal cords do the same thing. You can also create sound

You Will Need

- **AN ADULT**
- **bottles with narrow necks**
- **6 or 7 marbles of the same size**
- **grooved ruler**
- **5 to 6 people**
- **Slinky® spring toy**
- **smooth floor**
- **a partner**
- **matches**
- **candle**
- **candleholder**
- **empty one-gallon plastic milk jug**
- **heavy spoon**
- **kitchen sink with light over it**
- **cork or other small floating object**

waves by blowing across a bottle with a narrow neck. The air in the bottle will vibrate and produce sound waves that travel through the air. This is the way wind instruments, such as the flute and trumpet, create musical notes.

1. To make a sound with a narrow-neck bottle, such as a soda bottle, hold the bottle in a vertical position. Push the top of the bottle firmly against your lower lip. Blow air gently across the mouth of the bottle. You will hear a distinct low-pitched sound.

2. Repeat the experiment with narrow-neck bottles of different sizes. How is the length of the bottle related to the pitch of the sound coming from the bottle?

3. To see how a sound wave travels through air, place six or seven marbles of the same size side by side on a grooved ruler. The marbles represent molecules of air. Pull one marble aside and roll it against the others. Watch the motion travel through the marbles and emerge at the opposite end as the last marble rolls away from the others. In air, the molecules are far apart, but the motion of the wave is similar.

4. Here is another way to illustrate how sound waves travel: Ask five or six people to stand in a line, one behind the other a

little less than an arm's length apart. Have everyone put their hands firmly against the person in front of them. The person at the head of the line has no one to push against. He or she should be ready to step forward when pushed. Give the person at the end of the line a gentle push on the back and watch what happens.

Although molecules of air are far apart, they do bump into one another as they transport sound outward from its source. The movement of the sound waves is similar to what you saw with marbles and people.

5. A good model of sound waves can be seen with a Slinky® spring toy. Place the Slinky on a smooth floor. Have a partner hold one end of it. Grab the other end and stretch the Slinky out across the floor as shown in Figure 2a. Compress your end of the Slinky by quickly pushing it toward your partner and then quickly pulling it back. You will see the pulse (the compressed portion of the spring) travel down the Slinky. Then it will be reflected back—just as a sound is often reflected as an echo.

6. Move your end of the Slinky back and forth, toward you and then toward your partner (not side to side), to create a series

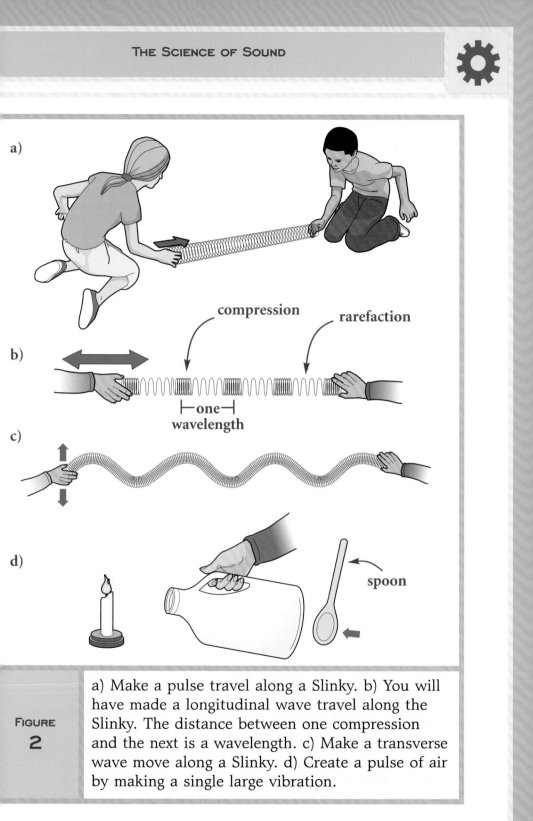

a) compression   rarefaction

b) ⊢one⊣
wavelength

c)

d) spoon

FIGURE 2

a) Make a pulse travel along a Slinky. b) You will have made a longitudinal wave travel along the Slinky. The distance between one compression and the next is a wavelength. c) Make a transverse wave move along a Slinky. d) Create a pulse of air by making a single large vibration.

of equally spaced pulses. You have created waves on the Slinky. Regions of the Slinky where the coils are close together are called compressions. Regions where the coils are farther apart are called rarefactions. The waves you made are called longitudinal waves. The particles in a longitudinal wave (the coils of the Slinky or air molecules in a sound wave) move back and forth along the same path that the waves travel (Figure 2b).

7. Move your end of the Slinky sideways instead of forward and back. Do this repeatedly and you will see transverse waves like those in Figure 2c. Notice that the Slinky moves perpendicularly (at right angles) to the direction that the wave travels. Water waves and light waves are also examples of transverse waves.

In sound waves, which are longitudinal waves, where the air molecules are pushed closer together, there is a region of compression. Where the molecules are far apart, there is a region of rarefaction. The vibrating object pushes air molecules together as it moves one way and leaves air molecules farther apart when it moves the opposite way.

8. To see the effect of a single sound pulse, **ask an adult** to light a candle in a candleholder. Hold an empty one-gallon plastic milk jug about a foot from the flame. Point its mouth at the flame. Bang hard on the bottom of the jug with a heavy spoon (Figure 2d). Why do you think the flame goes out?

   Another way to understand how sound waves travel is to watch water waves. Unlike sound waves, which move longitudinally, water waves are transverse waves.

9. Turn on a light over a kitchen sink. Fill the sink with about an inch of water. When the water has stopped moving, dip your finger into the center of the water. Watch the wave pulse move. See how it bounces back (reflects) when it hits the side of the sink?

   Dip your finger again and again. Watch the waves that you generate. This is similar to how sound waves from a vibrating object move through air.

   The movement of sound waves through air is similar to waves traveling through water. However, sound waves are longitudinal. They form as air molecules move together and apart. Water waves are transverse. The water molecules move up and down, perpendicular to the direction of the wave.

SOUND PROJECTS WITH A MUSIC LAB YOU CAN BUILD

The waves you made with your finger moved outward to the sides of the sink. The waves were reflected back toward the center of the sink. The same thing happens when you hear an echo. Sound waves are reflected from a hard surface such as a brick wall and come back toward their source.

10. Make some more waves with your finger. To see that it is the wave that travels and not the water, place a cork or any small object that floats on the water. Then generate some waves. As you can see, the floating object bobs up and down as waves pass, but it does not move with the wave. The same thing happens with sound waves. The air molecules move back and forth, but they do not move along with the wave.

IDEAS FOR YOUR SCIENCE FAIR

• Design and carry out different ways to measure the speed of sound in air. How do your results compare with the speed given above? Which method of measuring the speed of sound is the most accurate?

• How does temperature affect the speed of sound in air? Do experiments to find out.

A SOUND TRUMPET

Before hearing aids were invented, people who were slightly deaf used sound trumpets. You can make a sound trumpet very easily.

1. Roll a large sheet of heavy paper or light cardboard into the shape of a cone. Use tape to hold the cone together. One end of the cone should be very wide. The other end should be quite narrow to fit against, but not in, your ear.

2. Hold the narrow end of the trumpet against your ear. Turn the wide end toward a soft sound on the other side of the room, such as a radio with its volume turned low. Notice how the trumpet captures and reflects sound waves into your ear.

   If you speak or shout into the narrow end of the trumpet, you have a megaphone. The sound waves from your mouth will be reflected by the trumpet walls and sent in a particular direction.

3. Notice how much better someone can hear you when you point the megaphone toward them and speak into it.

You Will Need

- **large sheet of heavy paper or light cardboard**
- **tape**

SOUND IN SOLIDS AND LIQUIDS

Y ou know that sound waves move through air. They also move through other gases. They travel faster in gases less dense (lighter) than air and slower in gases more dense (heavier) than air. In hydrogen, which is about one-fourteenth as dense as air, sounds travel at 2,860 mph (4,600 km/hr). In carbon dioxide, which is about $1^1/2$ times as dense as air, the speed of sound is 580 mph (930 km/hr).

Will sound waves travel through solids and liquids?

1. To find out, place the back of a watch that ticks each second at one end of a wooden table. Place your ear firmly against the other end of the table (Figure 3a). Can you hear the watch ticking? If not, how close must you move your ear to hear the watch? Can you hear it ticking through the air at the same distance? Does sound travel better through wood or through air?

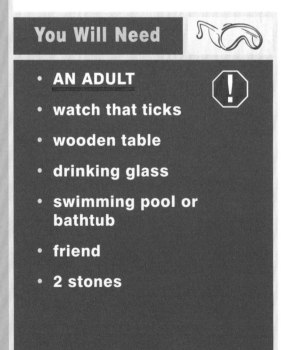

You Will Need

- **AN ADULT** !
- **watch that ticks**
- **wooden table**
- **drinking glass**
- **swimming pool or bathtub**
- **friend**
- **2 stones**

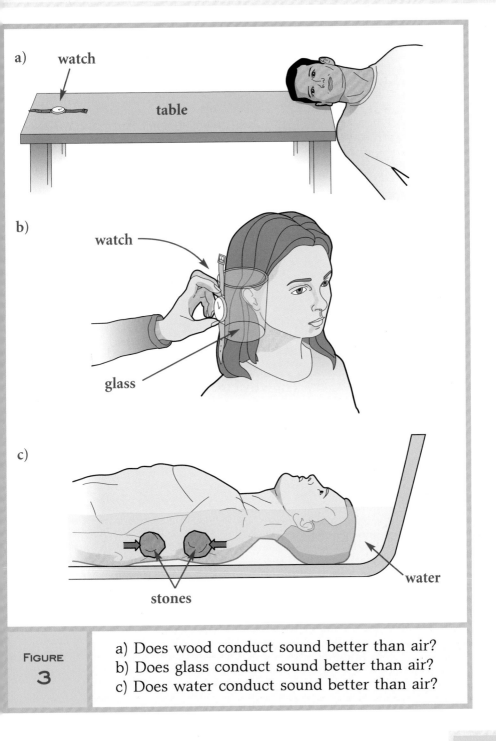

a) watch

table

b) watch

glass

c)

stones

water

FIGURE 3

a) Does wood conduct sound better than air?
b) Does glass conduct sound better than air?
c) Does water conduct sound better than air?

2. Place a drinking glass firmly against your ear. Hold the back of the watch against the other side of the glass (Figure 3b). Can you hear the ticking? Remove the glass but keep the watch at the same place. Can you hear better through glass or through air?

3. Next time you go swimming, stand in the shallow part of the water. Hold your breath and put your head under water. Have a friend tap two stones together under the water. Then, with your head above water, have your friend tap the stones together in air at the same distance from you. Does sound travel through water? Does it travel better through water or through air?

    You can do a similar experiment in your bathtub **under adult supervision** (Figure 3c).

    Table 1 gives the speed of sound in some different liquids and solids. How does the speed of sound in solids compare with the speed of sound in liquids? With the speed of sound in gases?

TABLE I	The speed of sound in some liquids and solids at room temperature (77°F, or 25°C)		
Liquid or solid	Speed (miles/hour)	Speed (meters/sec)	Speed (km/hour)
alcohol (ethanol)	2,700	1,207	4,345
brass	10,510	4,700	16,920
glass (Pyrex)	12,610	5,640	20,300
granite	8,830	3,950	14,220
iron	13,300	5,950	21,420
water	3,345	1,496	5,385

IDEAS FOR YOUR SCIENCE FAIR

- Is the speed of sound related to the density of the substance through which it travels? If it is, can you find a way of relating it mathematically?

- Do an experiment to show that sound cannot travel in a vacuum.

- Make a model to show how sound is transmitted through the human ear.

SCIENCE AND MUSIC

T here is a **close connection** between science and music. Many scientists play musical instruments. Many musicians are interested in the science needed to understand music and the particular instrument they play.

Pythagoras was an ancient Greek mathematician and scientist who lived before 500 B.C.E. He was the first person to connect science with music. Pythagoras introduced the idea of an octave. He discovered that certain combinations of frequencies (notes) are pleasant or unpleasant to the human ear. He also discovered that if he shortened the length of the string of a musical instrument, the string's pitch (frequency) became higher. In fact, if he halved the length, the pitch doubled. This is what led him to the idea of an octave. If a certain note has a frequency of 440 Hz, a note one octave higher will have a frequency twice as high, or 880 Hz. A note an octave lower will have a frequency half as high, or 220 Hz.

The first experiment in this chapter is similar to an experiment that Pythagoras did more than 2,500 years ago.

THE SCIENCE OF STRINGS

1. **Find a 1-in × 6-in (2.5-cm × 15-cm) board** approximately 18 in (46 cm) long. Fasten it to an old table or bench with a C-clamp as shown in Figure 4. Let one end of the board extend about 6 in (15 cm) beyond the table or bench.

2. Mark two points about 1 inch from the side and end of the board on the table. Hammer a nail a short distance into these points and then remove the nail. The small holes will make it easier to insert two screw eyes into the board, as shown. If you have difficulty turning the screw eyes, put the blade end of

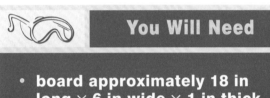

You Will Need

- **board approximately 18 in long × 6 in wide × 1 in thick (46 cm × 15 cm × 2.5 cm)**
- **yardstick or meterstick**
- **old table or bench**
- **C-clamp**
- **hammer**
- **nail**
- **2 screw eyes without gaps in the eyes**
- **screwdriver (optional)**
- **scissors**
- **50-pound– and 30-pound-test monofilament fishing line**
- **2 empty half-gallon plastic bleach bottles or sand pails that are about the same weight**
- **measuring cup**
- **water**
- **pencil**

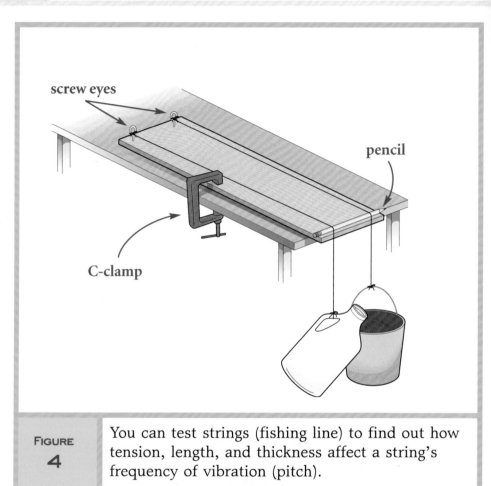

| FIGURE 4 | You can test strings (fishing line) to find out how tension, length, and thickness affect a string's frequency of vibration (pitch). |

a small screwdriver or the sharp end of the nail into the eye. Use the other end of the screwdriver or nail to wind the screw eye.

3. Cut two pieces of 50-pound-test monofilament fishing line, each about 30 in (75 cm) long. Tie one end of each line to a screw eye. Tie the other end of each line to the handle of an

empty half-gallon plastic bleach bottle or sand pail. Both containers should have the same weight.

4. Add four cups of water to both bottles or pails. Place a pencil under the lines near the end of the board as shown. Pluck each line with your finger. The two sounds should have very nearly the same pitch (frequency).

5. Add four more cups of water to one of the bottles or pails. This will increase the stretching force or pull (tension) on one of the strings. Again, pluck each string. How does increasing the tension on a string affect its pitch, or frequency of vibration?

6. Use a finger to hold the center of one string against the board. This makes the string half as long. Pluck the shortened string. How does shortening the string affect its pitch? How does lengthening the string affect its pitch?

7. Empty the water from the bottles or pails. Then replace one of the strings with 30-pound-test monofilament fishing line. It should be the same length as the 50-pound line. Put eight cups of water into each bottle or pail so that both strings will be under the same tension. Notice that the 30-pound-test line is not as thick as the 50-pound-test line. Now pluck first

one string and then the other. Do the strings have the same frequency, or does one vibrate with a higher frequency than the other?

How does the thickness of a string affect the frequency at which it vibrates?

Can you adjust the lengths of the two different strings so that they produce the same note (frequency)? If you can, which string has the greater length?

1. **Tie one end of a long jump rope** or a length of clothesline to a rigid support such as a doorknob or a post. Hold the free end of the rope and extend it to its full length by walking away from the fixed end.

   By moving your hand up and down, you can send waves to the fixed end of the rope. If you send one wave and stop, you will see that pulse reflected from the fixed end. How does increasing the tension in the rope affect the speed at which the wave moves?

2. Move your hand in a circle the way you would if you were turning the rope for someone to jump rope. You now have a three-dimensional wave. The waves you made on a slinky were two-dimensional: they only moved from side to side or back and forth. The three-dimensional wave you have made is like a standing wave. Standing waves form when incoming waves meet previous waves that have been reflected. Because the waves cancel one another at half wave-length intervals, they form

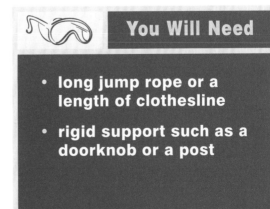

You Will Need

- **long jump rope or a length of clothesline**
- **rigid support such as a doorknob or a post**

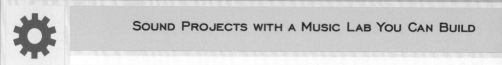
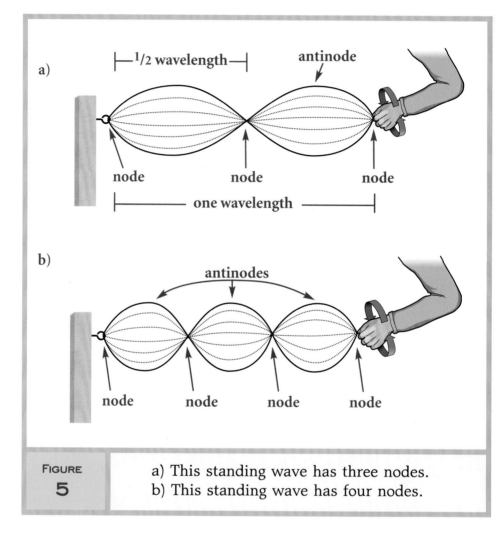

a)

├─¹/₂ wavelength─┤

antinode

node   node   node

├──────── one wavelength ────────┤

b)

antinodes

node   node   node   node

| FIGURE 5 | a) This standing wave has three nodes. b) This standing wave has four nodes. |

nodes (points where there is no wave movement). The waves you are making have two nodes (points that do not move), one at each end. The part in the middle, which sweeps out an oval-shaped space, is called an antinode. The distance between the two nodes is half a wavelength.

3. If you spin the rope twice as fast, you will produce a node in the middle as well as the nodes at each end (see Figure 5a). You will then have a complete but shorter wavelength between your hand and the fixed end of the rope.

4. Can you spin the rope fast enough to produce four nodes? If you can, you will see $1\frac{1}{2}$ wavelengths between your hand and the fixed end of the rope (Figure 5b).

When the string of a musical instrument is plucked or bowed, standing waves form on the string. The string vibrates as a whole. It has two nodes, one at each end, as shown in Figure 6a, so that the distance between the nodes is half a wavelength. This is called the string's fundamental frequency, or first harmonic. However, the string vibrating at its fundamental frequency may have other frequencies superimposed on it. For example, in Figure 6b, you see a string vibrating at its fundamental frequency. At the same time,

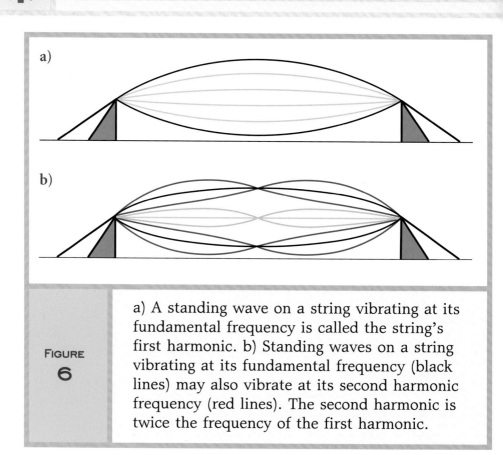

a)

b)

FIGURE 6

a) A standing wave on a string vibrating at its fundamental frequency is called the string's first harmonic. b) Standing waves on a string vibrating at its fundamental frequency (black lines) may also vibrate at its second harmonic frequency (red lines). The second harmonic is twice the frequency of the first harmonic.

it is also vibrating at twice that frequency, creating a node at the center of the string. This second vibration, superimposed on the fundamental frequency, is called the second harmonic. It vibrates at twice the fundamental frequency. There may even be third and fourth harmonics with frequencies three and four times the fundamental frequency. This makes a very rich sound. These harmonics are often called overtones.

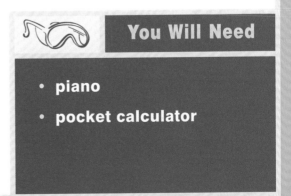

Pythagoras was the first scientist to recognize that shortening a string increases the frequency at which it vibrates. In fact, halving a string's length doubles its frequency, making its pitch an octave higher.

Pythagoras found that hearing two frequencies (pitches) at the same time could be pleasing (concordant) or displeasing (discordant) to the ear. He found that two notes one octave apart (a frequency ratio of 2:1) when played together sound harmonious and concordant. Other combinations of frequencies that are small whole-number ratios, such as 3:2 or 4:3, are also concordant. Larger whole-number ratios such as 9:8 are discordant.

If you can play the piano, or know the keys on a piano, you can do this experiment easily. If not, use Figure 7 to help find the notes you need to play. Middle C, with a frequency of 261.6 Hz, is shown in Figure 7. Starting from the left end of the keyboard, middle C is the white key just before the fourth set of double black keys on

You Will Need

- **piano**
- **pocket calculator**

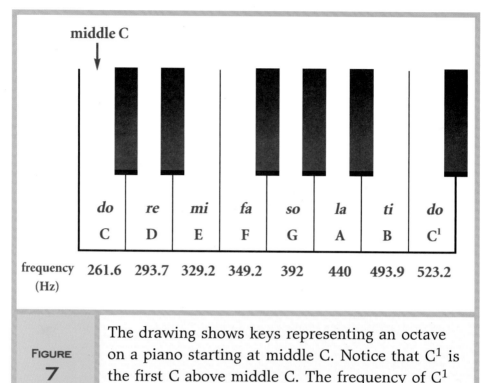

middle C

do	re	mi	fa	so	la	ti	do
C	D	E	F	G	A	B	C¹

frequency (Hz) 261.6 293.7 329.2 349.2 392 440 493.9 523.2

FIGURE 7

The drawing shows keys representing an octave on a piano starting at middle C. Notice that C^1 is the first C above middle C. The frequency of C^1 is twice that of middle C ($261.6 \times 2 = 523.2$).

the keyboard. You may have heard someone sing an octave as "*do, re, mi, fa, so, la, ti, do.*" Those sung notes may correspond to the keys C, D, E, F, G A, B, C^1 on the piano.

From the diagram of the piano keys and their frequencies (Figure 7), which combinations of two notes played together would you expect to sound harmonious? Which combinations of notes would you expect to sound discordant? A pocket calculator will help you to find ratios. For example, the ratio of C^1 to middle C is $523.2 \div 261.6 = 2$ or 2:1. The ratio of G to C is $392 \div 261.6 = 1.498$, which is very close to 1.5, or 3:2. (Remember to convert your ratios to whole numbers.)

Listen to each combination as it is played. Did you predict each combination correctly?

IDEA FOR YOUR SCIENCE FAIR

Two or more notes played at the same time constitute a chord. A two-note chord is called a dyad; a three-note chord is called a triad; a four-note chord is called a tetrad. Play chords of all types. Which are harmonious? Which are discordant?

A STRING TELEPHONE AND A "BELL"

Strings can carry (conduct) sounds as well as make them. Do you think strings can conduct the sounds made by your voice?

1. To find out, obtain two clean, empty, 10-oz or larger metal food cans. Use a hammer and a small finishing nail to make a hole in the bottom of both cans. Connect the cans with a heavy string about 15 ft (4.5 m) long. Tie a paper clip to each end of the string so that it cannot slip out of the cans.

2. Have a partner hold one can while you hold the other. Pull the cans as far apart as possible so that the string is tight. Have your partner whisper into one can while you hold the other can against your ear. Can you hear what your partner is saying? Can he or she hear you when you whisper into the can you hold? Do you think you will be able to

You Will Need

- **clean empty soup cans of different sizes**
- **hammer**
- **small finishing nail**
- **heavy string**
- **2 paper clips**
- **meterstick or yardstick**
- **a partner**
- **a staircase**
- **a dining fork**

hear better or less well if the string is not tight? What makes you think so? Try it! Was your prediction correct?

3. Repeat the experiment, but this time use larger cans. Do you think the size of the can will affect how well you can hear your partner's message? What makes you think so? Why should the string be tight and its length be the same as before?

   If the size of the can makes a difference, do you think both cans need to be that size? If not, is it the can spoken into or the one listened to that has to be a particular size?

4. Predict what will happen to the sounds you hear if you pinch the tight string leading to the can. Try it! Were you right?

5. Do you think it matters whether or not the string is level? For instance, would you be able to hear as well if you were at the top of a staircase and your partner was at the bottom? Try it! What do you find?

6. What about corners? Do you think your telephone will work around a corner? Try it! Were you right?

   Here is another illustration of how sound can be carried on a string.

7. Tie a dining fork at the center of a long piece of heavy string.

Gently strike the fork against the edge of a table and listen to the sound it makes. Now put the ends of the string in your ears and hold them there with your index fingers. Again, gently strike the fork against the edge of a table and listen to the bell-like sound it makes.

Does sound travel better through the solid string or through air? Can you detect sounds through the string that you did not hear through the air? Where have you heard such sounds before?

8. Remove the string from the dining fork. Pluck the tines of the fork. Can you hear the sound if you place the tines near your ear? Repeat the experiment, but this time put the handle of the fork between your teeth after you pluck the tines. Does sound travel better through bone or through air?

IDEAS FOR YOUR SCIENCE FAIR

- Figure out a way to make a conference call on a string telephone; that is, connect a number of "phones" to allow several people to listen and talk to the same person.
- Do experiments to see whether the thickness or length of the string affects your ability to hear on a string telephone.

A VIBRATING AIR COLUMN

rchestras are made up of large sections of instruments, including woodwinds and brass. Woodwinds include flutes, piccolos, clarinets, oboes, and bassoons. Brass instruments include French horns, trumpets, trombones, tubas, and cornets. Woodwinds and brass instruments produce notes of different pitches by making air vibrate in columns of different lengths.

1. To see the basic principle involved in a woodwind or brass instrument, you will need a piece of plastic tubing. It should be about 6 in (15 cm) long with an inside diameter of $^1/_2$ to $^3/_4$ in (1.5 cm to 2 cm).

2. Find a bolt that is nearly the same length as the tubing, along with two nuts that fit the bolt and can move freely inside the tubing.

3. Next, obtain a washer with the same diameter as the inside of the tubing. Use the two nuts to hold the

You Will Need

- **plastic tubing about 6 in (15 cm) long with an inside diameter of $^1/_2$ in to $^3/_4$ in (1.5 cm to 2 cm)**
- **long bolt**
- **2 nuts that fit the bolt and fit inside the tubing**
- **washer with the same diameter as the inside of the tubing**
- **petroleum jelly**

washer in place at a point near the end of the bolt, as shown in Figure 8. Add a little petroleum jelly to the edge of the washer. The lubricant will allow you to move the washer more easily along the plastic tube.

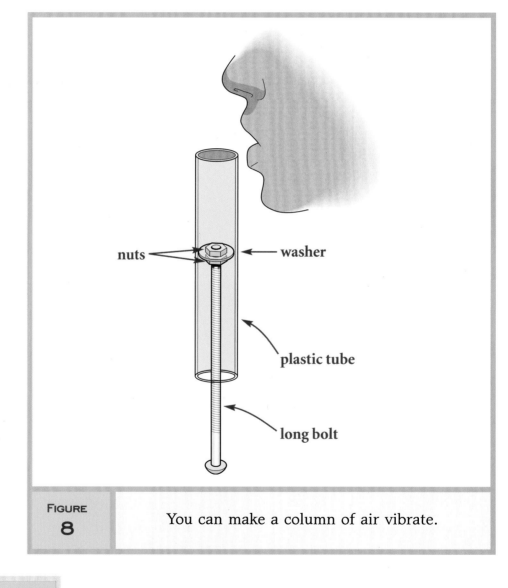

FIGURE 8

You can make a column of air vibrate.

4. Insert the bolt and its washer into the tube. Use the bolt to position the washer about one-third of the way up the tube.

5. Place your lower lip against the upper edge of the tube and blow air across the tube. Note the pitch of the sound you hear.

6. Next, use the bolt to shorten the length of the air column. Place the washer about halfway up the tube. Again, blow into the tube. Is the pitch higher or lower than the sound you heard when the air column was longer?

7. Finally, shorten the air column some more by placing the washer about two-thirds of the way up the tube. Predict the pitch of the sound you will hear when you blow into the shorter air column. Will the pitch be higher or lower than before? Again, blow into the tube. Was your prediction correct?

How does the length of an air column affect the pitch of the sound it makes when it vibrates?

IDEA FOR YOUR SCIENCE FAIR

Use what you have learned in this experiment to make a woodwind instrument on which you can play simple tunes.

RESONANCE

Vibrating objects, such as strings and air columns, have natural frequencies. For example, the A key on a piano strikes a string that vibrates at 440 Hz. If you sing a note that has a frequency of 440 Hz, that piano string will respond and vibrate at its natural frequency of 440 Hz. The vibrational response of any object to its natural frequency is called resonance.

A playground swing has a natural frequency that depends on the length of the swing, not on the weight of the person seated on the swing. If you push someone on a swing each time the swing begins to move from the highest point of its motion, the swing will move higher with each push. You are

You Will Need

- **scissors**
- **ruler**
- **construction paper**
- **tape**
- **cardboard**
- **two 1-L plastic soda bottles**
- **piano**
- **a partner**
- **2-L plastic bottle**
- **tall vase**
- **sink**
- **open cylinder, such as a mailing tube, that will fit inside the vase**
- **tuning fork**

making the swing resonate. Of course, you could also make the swing resonate by pushing it every other swing or every third or fourth swing. You could also make it resonate by having a partner push at the other end of the swing's to-and-fro motion. The push frequency would just be twice that of the swing's frequency. A piano string receiving sound waves at its natural frequency from another source will vibrate farther and its sound will grow louder. This will also be true if the sound waves have a frequency that is half or twice the natural frequency of the string.

1. You can demonstrate resonance with a mechanical model. To do this, make some paper rings. Using scissors, cut 1-in– (2.5-cm–) wide strips from construction paper. The longest one should be about 20 in (50 cm) long. (Long strips can be made by taping shorter strips together.) Make other strips that are about 16, 12, and 6 in (40, 30, and 15 cm) long. Tape the ends of each strip together to make rings. Then tape the rings to a sheet of cardboard as shown in Figure 9.

2. Move the cardboard slowly and smoothly back and forth from side to side at very low but increasing frequency. Watch the largest ring. It will be the first to resonate. It will move

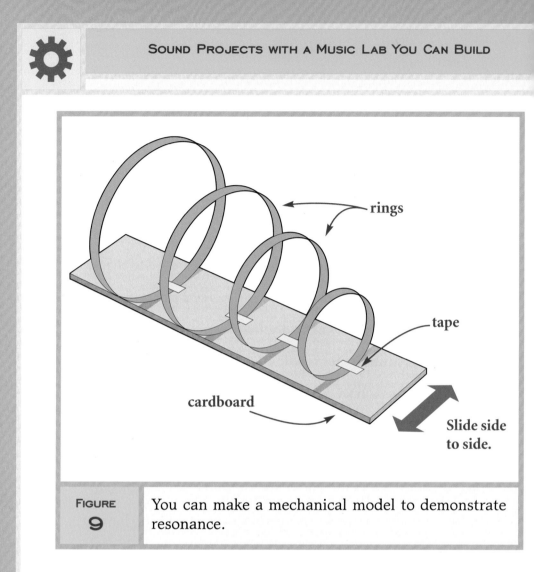

FIGURE 9 You can make a mechanical model to demonstrate resonance.

back and forth at the same frequency as the cardboard you are moving. (Other rings may move but not as much.) Slowly increase the frequency at which you move the cardboard back and forth. Each ring, in turn, will resonate to a particular frequency. Do you think the rings will resonate to an up-and-down motion of the cardboard? Try it! Were you right?

3. Open a piano. Use your foot to hold down the pedal on the right (the sustaining pedal). This lifts the dampers so that the strings can vibrate freely. Sing a note loudly and clearly. Then listen carefully. You will hear sounds coming from the strings that resonate to the note you sang.

4. Resonance can also be found in a vibrating column of air. To see that this is true, put your lower lip against the edge of the mouth of an empty 1-L plastic soda bottle. Blow air across the mouth of the bottle. You should hear a low-pitched sound caused by air vibrating in the bottle.

5. Hold the same bottle next to your ear. Have a partner blow across the mouth of an identical bottle. What do you hear coming from your bottle? What does your friend hear when you blow into your bottle?

6. Repeat the experiment, but this time have your partner blow across the mouth of a 2-L plastic bottle while you listen with a 1-L bottle. What is different this time? How do the sounds made with the 1-L and 2-L bottles differ?

7. Find a tall vase and an open cylinder such as a used mailing tube that will fit inside the vase. Fill the vase with water and leave it in the sink. Place the mailing tube in the water.

The water level in the tube will match the level in the vase. Now hold a vibrating tuning fork with a frequency of 512 Hz just above the upper end of the mailing tube. Sound waves from the tuning fork go down the tube and will be reflected by the water. Move the mailing tube and tuning fork up and down together. You will find a position or positions where resonance is evident (the sound will suddenly grow louder).

IDEA FOR YOUR SCIENCE FAIR

Using what you know about vibrating air columns, sound, and the speed of sound in air, design and carry out an experiment to find the wavelength of the sound made by a tuning fork of a particular frequency. Bear in mind that the wavelength of a sound wave is equal to its speed divided by its frequency.

Y ou may have heard someone say that you can hear the sounds of the sea by holding a conch shell against your ear. In fact, you can hear such sounds, but the sounds are not really of the sea.

1. Hold an empty mailing tube open at both ends against your ear. The air in the tube resonates to any sounds that match its natural frequency of vibration.

2. Hold mailing tubes of different lengths against your ear, and you will find that the pitch of the sound you hear differs. The longer the tube, the lower the pitch of the sound.

3. While listening to the resonance of a sound in a mailing tube held against your ear, move the tube a very short distance from your ear so that the tube is no longer touching your ear, and is open at both ends. What happens to the pitch of the sound you hear?

IDEA FOR YOUR SCIENCE FAIR

Carry out an investigation to find out why the pitch of the resonant sound heard in a mailing tube increases when you move it a short distance from your ear.

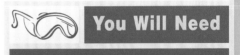

You Will Need

- **wide mailing tubes of different lengths, open at both ends**

INSTRUMENTS WITH STRINGS

The stringed instruments you see in an orchestra or band, such as violins, violas, cellos, basses, guitars, and banjos, have a number of common features. The instruments have strings and a long neck connected to a hollow part that has an opening under the strings. The strings vary in thickness. They are attached near the end of the hollow part and to pegs near the end of the long neck. The strings run over a bridge that holds them up and keeps them separated. The musician can use his or her fingers to press the strings onto the neck. This will shorten the strings and change the pitch of the note produced by the strings when plucked or bowed.

Tension in the strings can be changed by turning the pegs. Musicians use the pegs to tune their stringed instruments. You will see violinists and cellists both pluck and bow. Banjos and mandolins are always plucked either with a finger or a pick. Guitars are plucked or strummed.

Other stringed instruments, such as the harp and piano, are built differently. Like the guitar, though, the strings of the harp are plucked or strummed. Piano strings are struck with soft covered mallets that are connected to the keys on the keyboard.

WHAT IS THE PURPOSE OF A MUTE ON A STRINGED INSTRUMENT?

1. **Find a large empty coffee** can with a plastic lid. Use large scissors to cut out a piece of corrugated cardboard about 1 1/2 inches (4 cm) × 3 inches (8 cm).

2. **Ask an adult** to score the middle of the cardboard strip with a sharp knife. Then fold the strip to make a bridge on top of the plastic cover, as shown in Figure 10.

3. Stretch a rubber band over the can and bridge as shown. Pluck the "string" (rubber band) and listen to the sound.

4. Next, clip a mute (clothespin) to the bridge as shown. Again, pluck the string. What has the mute done to the sound of the plucked string?

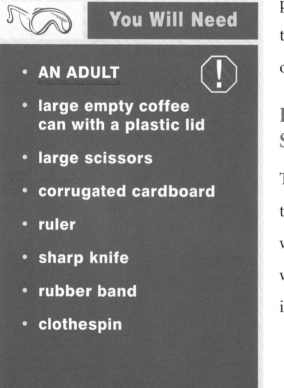

You Will Need

- **AN ADULT**
- **large empty coffee can with a plastic lid**
- **large scissors**
- **corrugated cardboard**
- **ruler**
- **sharp knife**
- **rubber band**
- **clothespin**

IDEA FOR YOUR SCIENCE FAIR

Talk to a violinist about the use of a mute. Ask when it is used it and why. Investigate how other instruments are muted.

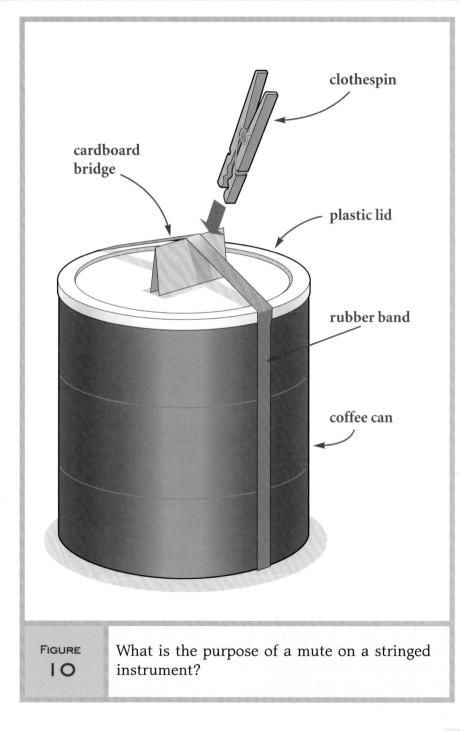

clothespin

cardboard bridge

plastic lid

rubber band

coffee can

FIGURE
10

What is the purpose of a mute on a stringed instrument?

WHY IS THERE A HOLLOW BOX UNDER THE STRINGS?

You may wonder why stringed instruments, such as a violin, have a hollow wooden portion under the strings.

1. To see why they do, stretch out a rubber band and pluck it. Then put the same rubber band around an open box, such as a shoebox. Again, pluck the rubber band. In which case was the sound louder?

2. Strike a tine of a tuning fork by tapping it with a mallet that may have come with the tuning fork, or you can tap it against the rubber heel of your shoe. The sound produced by the vibrating tines of the tuning fork will have a constant frequency.

3. Strike the tuning fork again. This time, hold the base of the tuning fork against a wooden table. Is the sound louder than it was before? If it is, can you explain what makes it louder?

Why do you think the hollow portion beneath the strings of a violin is called a sound box?

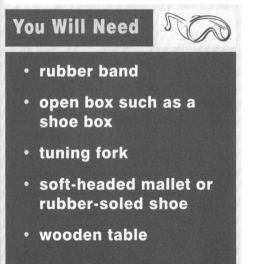

You Will Need

- **rubber band**
- **open box such as a shoe box**
- **tuning fork**
- **soft-headed mallet or rubber-soled shoe**
- **wooden table**

A WIDE-KEYED "PIANO"

Real pianos have 88 keys that cause soft hammers to strike strings and produce musical frequencies that have a range of 7¹/₂ octaves. You can make a much less complicated piano with only eight keys that you can pluck.

1. Place eight jumbo craft sticks or tongue depressors along the edge of an old table, bench, or workbench. Place a wooden block across the ends of the sticks. Arrange the sticks so that each one extends less beyond the edge than the previous one. Use two C-clamps to hold the wooden block firmly against the sticks, as shown in Figure 11.

2. Pluck each key (tongue depressor) and listen to the sound it makes. How does the length of the keys affect the frequency of the sounds they make?

3. To make a full scale—*do, re, mi, fa, so, la, ti, do*¹— you will probably have to loosen the clamps slightly and adjust the lengths that

You Will Need

- **8 jumbo craft sticks, about 6 in × ³/₄ in (15 cm × 2 cm) or tongue depressors**

- **old table, bench, or workbench**

- **wooden block**

- **2 C-clamps**

extend beyond the edge of the table. Once you can play a full scale, see if you can play some simple tunes with your piano.

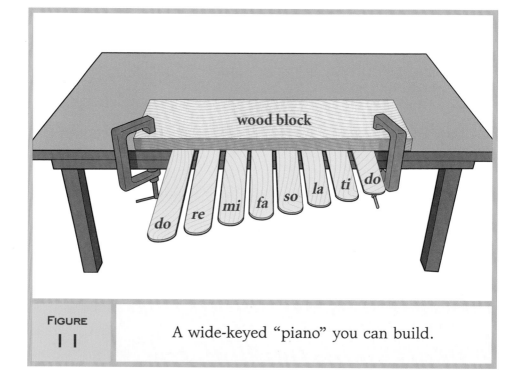

FIGURE
11

A wide-keyed "piano" you can build.

A TWANGY "PIANO"

1. **Ask an adult** to cut a wire coat hanger into eight pieces that vary in length from 6 in (15 cm) to 2 in (5 cm).

2. Place the wires of varying length along the edge of an old table, bench, or workbench. Lay a wooden block about 6 in long on the wires to hold them in place. To prevent cuts, cover the end of each wire with a small piece of masking tape.

3. Push down on the block with one hand while you pluck the wires with the thumb of your other hand. How would you expect the wire's length to affect the pitch of the sound it emits when plucked? Would longer wires produce sounds with a higher or a lower frequency?

4. Adjust the length of the wires until you can play a full scale—*do, re, mi, fa, so, la, ti, do*[1].

You Will Need

- **AN ADULT**
- **wire coat hanger**
- **wire cutter**
- **ruler**
- **old table, bench, or workbench**
- **wooden block about 6 in long**
- **masking tape**
- **hammer**
- **staples**

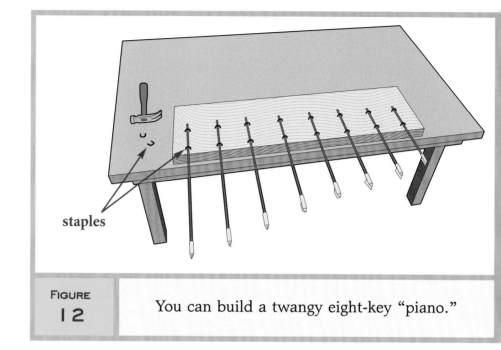

staples

FIGURE

12
You can build a twangy eight-key "piano."

Carefully measure the length of each wire. Then place the wires on the block. **Ask an adult** to hammer staples into the block to hold the wires in place with the proper lengths extending beyond the block, as shown in Figure 12.

Can you play some simple tunes with your twangy piano?

IDEA FOR YOUR SCIENCE FAIR

The twangy piano you made is also known as an African thumb piano. What is the origin of this instrument? Where and how is it used? What other materials can you use to make such a piano?

A ONE-STRING GUITAR

You can build a one-string guitar **under adult supervision**.

1. Find a ³/₄-in– (2-cm–) thick board about 24 in (60 cm) long and 2 in (5 cm) wide.

2. Insert a screw eye about a half inch from each end of the board. To insert a screw eye, hammer a nail a short distance into the board and then remove the nail. The small holes will make it easier to insert the screw eyes into the board. If you have difficulty turning the screw eyes, put the blade end of a

You Will Need

AN ADULT ⚠

³/₄-in– (2-cm–) thick board about 24 in (60 cm) long and 2 in (5 cm) wide

2 screw eyes without gaps in the eyes

ruler

hammer

nail

screwdriver (optional)

handsaw

- 2 craft sticks or popsicle sticks
- glue (optional)
- 50-pound-test monofilament fishing line
- scissors
- pen or pencil
- paper
- coin

small screwdriver or the sharp end of a nail into the eye. Use it to turn the screw eye.

3. **Ask an adult** to use a handsaw to make two $^1/_4$-inch– (6-mm–) deep grooves. Each groove should be about $1^1/_2$ in (3.8 cm) from the screw eyes at opposite ends of the board. Insert a craft stick or a popsicle stick into each groove. The sticks should fit the grooves tightly. A really tight fit may require gentle hammering to get them in place. The sticks will serve as bridges for the string that you will attach next. If the sticks are loose because the grooves are too wide, remove them and add some glue to each groove. Then reinsert the sticks and let the glue dry.

4. Tie one end of some 50-pound-test monofilament fishing line to one screw eye. Tie the other end as tightly as possible to the screw eye at the opposite end of the board. Tighten the line some more by using a screwdriver or nail to turn a screw eye. You now have a one-string guitar (Figure 13).

5. Pluck the string (fishing line) and listen to the sound it makes. What do you predict will happen to the pitch of the string if you tighten it? Try it! Were you right?

6. Use the finger of one hand to press the string against the

board about halfway between the two screw eyes. The length of the string between your finger and the screw eye is now half as long as it was. When you pluck the string will the pitch of the note be higher or lower than it was before? Try it! Were you right?

7. Use your finger to press the string against the board at different places. Pluck the string at each place. What happens to the pitch of the sound you make as the string is shortened?

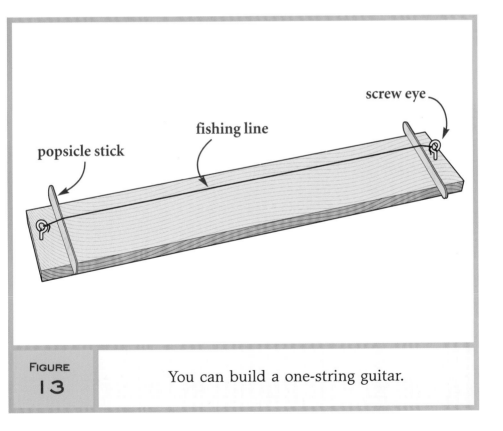

screw eye

fishing line

popsicle stick

FIGURE

13

You can build a one-string guitar.

See if you can produce a complete octave of notes—*do, re, mi, fa, so, la, ti, do*[1]—by pressing the string at different places. If you can, mark those places. Then try to play some simple tunes or write some tunes of your own. In place of notes, you could number the finger positions and simply use those numbers to write your music. Keep in mind that the string may loosen and need to be tuned frequently.

8. To make the notes sound louder, hold the back of the board against your ear as you pluck the string. Why do you think this makes the sound louder?

Will plucking the string with a pick (a coin will do nicely) rather than a finger change the sound?

A Two-String Bottle Banjo

1. Obtain a $3/4$-inch– (2-cm–) thick board about 2 in (5 cm) wide and 30 in (76 cm) long.

2. **Ask an adult** to use a sharp knife to cut an **H**-shaped slot (see Figure 14a) about an inch from the bottom of a 60-oz (1.77-L) plastic bottle, such as a clean, empty bleach bottle. The width and height of the slot should match the dimensions of the end of the board. An identical slot should be made on the opposite side of the bottle. Fold the **H** flaps outward (away from the bottle).

3. **Have the adult** also cut an opening about 2 in (5 cm) long and 1 in (2.5 cm) wide

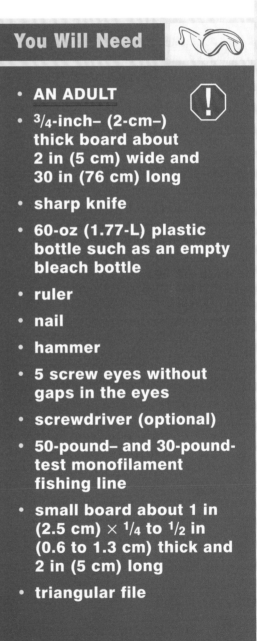

You Will Need

- **AN ADULT**
- **$3/4$-inch– (2-cm–) thick board about 2 in (5 cm) wide and 30 in (76 cm) long**
- **sharp knife**
- **60-oz (1.77-L) plastic bottle such as an empty bleach bottle**
- **ruler**
- **nail**
- **hammer**
- **5 screw eyes without gaps in the eyes**
- **screwdriver (optional)**
- **50-pound– and 30-pound-test monofilament fishing line**
- **small board about 1 in (2.5 cm) × $1/4$ to $1/2$ in (0.6 to 1.3 cm) thick and 2 in (5 cm) long**
- **triangular file**

a)

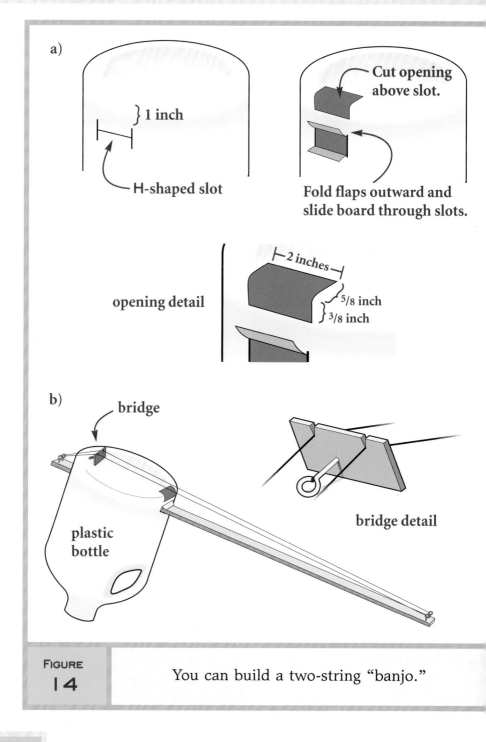

} 1 inch

H-shaped slot

Cut opening above slot.

Fold flaps outward and slide board through slots.

opening detail

|— 2 inches —|

} 5/8 inch
} 3/8 inch

b)

bridge

plastic bottle

bridge detail

FIGURE
14

You can build a two-string "banjo."

74

above one slot. The opening should extend about $3/8$ in (1 cm) up the side of the inverted bottle. The remaining $5/8$ in (1.6 cm) can be cut from the bottom of the bottle.

4. Slide one end of the board through the **H**-shaped slots. That end of the board should extend only about $2 1/2$ in (6.3 cm) beyond the bottle.

5. Use a nail and hammer to make two indentations about $1/2$ in (1.3 cm) from each end of the board. The indentations should be about 1 in (2.5 cm) apart. Use the indentations as starting holes for four screw eyes. As before, turn the screw eyes with a small screwdriver or nail.

6. Tie one end of some 50-pound-test monofilament fishing line to a screw eye at one end of the board.

7. Tie one end of some 30-pound-test monofilament fishing line to the other screw eye at the same end of the board. Extend the lines parallel to one another to the other end of the board. Tie them tightly to the screw eyes at that end.

8. Make a bridge for the strings from a small board about 1 in (2.5 cm) × $1/4$ to $1/2$ in (0.6 to 1.3 cm) thick and 2 in (5 cm) long. Insert a screw eye in the center of the small board so that it will stand upright in a slanting position on the bottom

of the bottle, as shown in Figure 14b. This will be the bridge. Use a triangular file to make two notches one inch apart in the top of the bridge. The notches will keep the strings apart and in proper position.

9. Use a screwdriver or nail to turn the screw eyes so that you can tune the banjo. If the strings are equally tight (under the same tension), which one will have a higher pitch when plucked? How do you know this? (Revisit Experiment 2-1 if you need a hint.)

10. Put your finger on the center of either string. Press the string against the board with your finger. Pluck the part of the string closer to the bottle. Then pluck the length of string farther from the bottle. Which end of the string made the louder sound when plucked? Can you explain why?

Can you obtain a full scale of notes by pressing each string against the board at different places with your finger? If you use both strings, can you obtain two octaves—from *do* to *do*^{1} to *do*^{2}?

Your "banjo" will look like this when it is built.

AN EIGHT-STRING HARP

1. **Obtain a board** 12 in (30 cm) by 15 in (38 cm) that is about $^1/_2$ in (1.3 cm) thick.

2. Using a pencil and ruler, draw a straight line across one of the short sides of the board about $^3/_4$ in (2 cm) from the edge. Along the line you drew, you should hammer in, part way, eight small nails with wide heads. Put the first nail in about $^3/_4$ in (2 cm) from the long edge of the board, as shown in Figure 15. Leave about $1^1/_2$ in (4 cm) between the nails. The last nail, like the first, should be about $^3/_4$ in (2 cm) from the long edge of the board.

3. Draw a second line on the board. This line should start $6^1/_2$ in (16.5 cm) above the last nail you

You Will Need

- **board 12 in × 15 in (30 cm × 43 cm) that is about $^1/_2$ in (1.3 cm) thick**
- **pencil**
- **ruler**
- **hammer**
- **8 small nails with wide heads**
- **8 screw eyes without gaps in the eyes**
- **long nail**
- **screwdriver (optional)**
- **50-pound-test monofilament fishing line**

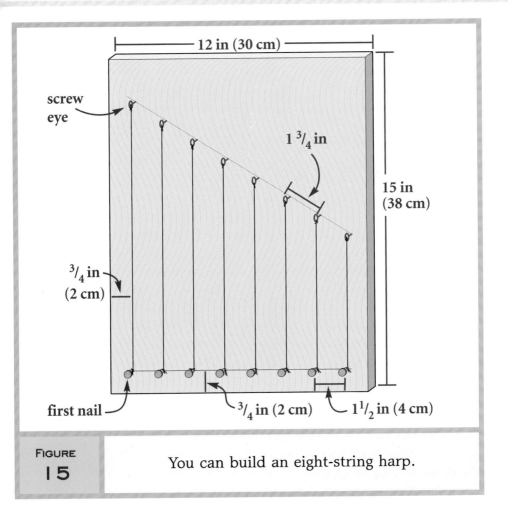

screw
eye

12 in (30 cm)

$1 \frac{3}{4}$ in

15 in
(38 cm)

$\frac{3}{4}$ in
(2 cm)

first nail

$\frac{3}{4}$ in (2 cm)

$1 \frac{1}{2}$ in (4 cm)

| FIGURE 15 | You can build an eight-string harp. |

drove into the board and extend to a point 13 in (33 cm) above the first nail you put in the board. The ends of the line should each be in 3/4 in (2 cm) from the long sides of the board.

4. Use a nail and hammer to make indentations at each end of the line you have just drawn. Use the indentations as starting

holes for two screw eyes. Turn the screw eyes, as before, with a small screwdriver or a nail. You should also make indentations to start six more screw eyes. These indentations should be equally spaced on the line between the two screw eyes. They should be in line with the nails you placed along the baseline. Therefore, they should be 1³/4 in (4.5 cm) apart along the slanted line, as shown in Figure 15. After making the indentations, insert the remaining six screw eyes.

5. Tie one end of a 50-pound-test monofilament fishing line to a nail at the base of the board. Tie the other end to the screw eye directly above it. Make the line as tight as possible. Repeat the process for each nail and corresponding screw eye, as shown in Figure 15. By turning the screw eyes with a small screwdriver or a long nail, you can tune the harp so that you can play a full scale on it.

6. To obtain a louder, richer sound, hold the board against your ear. Then pluck the strings on the other side of the board. Why do you think holding the board against your ear produces a louder, richer sound?

Can you play some simple tunes on your eight-string harp?

A "WASHTUB" BASS

1. **If you can find** an old metal washtub, **ask an adult** to drill a hole through the center of its bottom. If a washtub is not available, use a hammer and nail to make a hole through the center of the bottom of a child's metal sand pail or an empty paint bucket.

2. Thread one end of a 6-ft (1.8-m) length of twisted jute gardening twine (6-pound load limit works well) through the hole from outside the pail or tub to the inside (Figure 16). Tie a large knot in the end of the twine inside the tube so that it can't slide through the hole. If you can't make the knot big enough, tie the end of the twine to a clothespin or a short length of dowel.

You Will Need

- **AN ADULT** ⚠
- **metal washtub, sand pail, or empty paint bucket**
- **hammer**
- **nail**
- **drill and bit**
- **twisted jute gardening twine (6-pound load limit works well), about 6 ft (1.8 m) long**
- **2 clothespins or short lengths of dowel (optional)**
- **old broom handle or a 48-in (120-cm) length of 1-in– (2.5-cm–) diameter dowel**
- **triangular file**

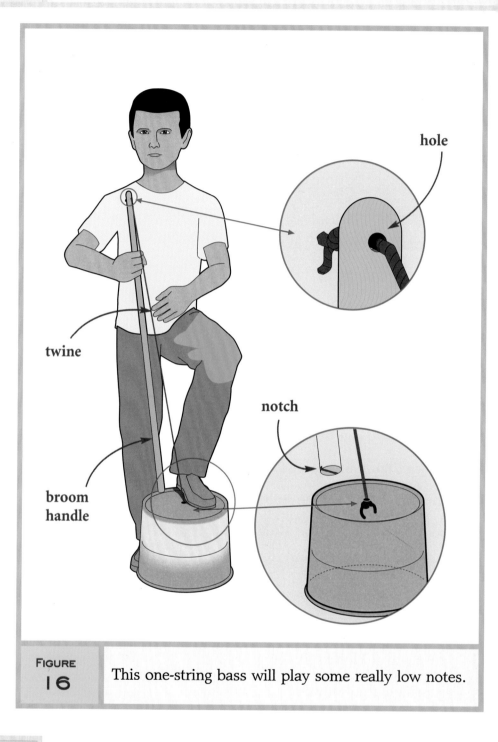

hole

twine

notch

broom
handle

Figure
16

This one-string bass will play some really low notes.

3. **Ask an adult** to drill a hole through one end of an old broom handle or a 48-in (120-cm) length of 1-in– (2.5-cm–) diameter dowel. The hole should be about 1-in– (2.5-cm–) from from the end of the handle or dowel. Use a triangular file to make a deep groove in the other end of the handle or dowel. The groove should be a quarter turn around the handle from the hole (perpendicular, or at a right angle, to the hole) that the adult drilled.

4. Put the groove at the end of the broom handle or dowel on the rim of the upside down pail or tub. Stand the dowel or broom handle upright on the pail or tub. Then thread the free end of the twine through the hole in the dowel or broom handle. Tie a large knot in the twine or tie it to a clothespin or short length of dowel so that it can't slip back through the hole. The twine extending from the top of the broom handle or dowel to the pail or tub should be taut (tight).

5. Put your foot on the pail or tub. Then tilt the broom handle or dowel outward to increase tension on the twine. Pluck the twine and you will hear the sound of a bass fiddle. To change the pitch of the sound, press the twine against the broom handle or dowel with the fingers of one hand. At the same

time, pluck the string with the fingers of the other hand. What do you think will happen to the pitch of the bass fiddle as you shorten the string? Try it! Were you right?

6. Predict what will happen to the pitch if you move the stick farther outward so as to increase the tension on the string. Try it! Did you predict correctly?

A Shoe Box Guitar

Fishing line or twine is not the only way to string a homemade instrument. You can build a simple guitar from a cardboard shoe box, pencils, and rubber-band "strings."

1. **Ask an adult** to use a sharp knife to cut a 3-in × 2 1/2-in (7.5-cm × 6.3-cm) opening in the top of a shoe box. The opening should be about 2 in (5 cm) from one end of the box.

2. Find about six rubber bands that have different widths. Stretch them around the box. All of them should lie above the opening in the box. Slide a pencil under the rubber bands at each end of the box, as shown in Figure 17.

   Which rubber band would you expect to have the highest pitch when plucked? Which rubber band would you expect to have the lowest pitch when plucked? Try it! Were you right?

   Tension in the rubber bands may differ when stretched around the box.

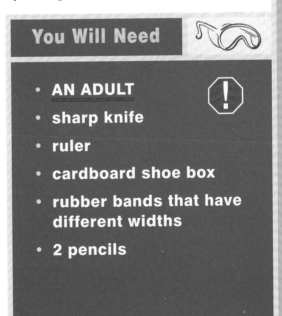

You Will Need

- **AN ADULT** (!)
- **sharp knife**
- **ruler**
- **cardboard shoe box**
- **rubber bands that have different widths**
- **2 pencils**

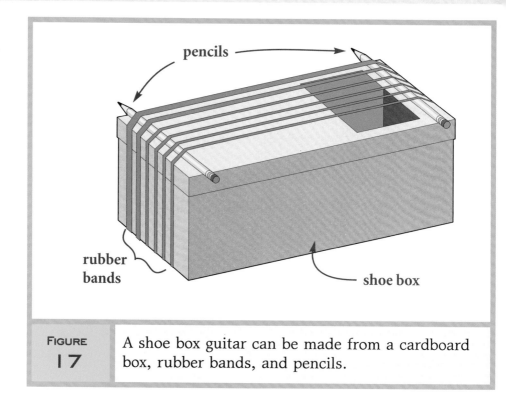

pencils

rubber
bands

shoe box

FIGURE 17	A shoe box guitar can be made from a cardboard box, rubber bands, and pencils.

Therefore, you may need to try a number of rubber bands until you get six that produce the frequencies you want when plucked. Arrange them in order according to pitch.

3. Use your fingers to press a string against the box. This will change the pitch produced by the "string" when plucked. How will shortening a string affect the pitch of the sound it emits?

Can you play some tunes on your shoe box guitar?

CHAPTER 4

WIND INSTRUMENTS

Wind instruments, as described in Experiment 2-5, are usually divided into two types, woodwinds and brasses. Woodwinds include such instruments as flutes, piccolos, clarinets, saxophones, and bassoons. Although they are called woodwinds, they do not have to be made of wood. Instruments such as French horns, trumpets, trombones, tubas, and cornets are classified as brass.

Wind instruments produce sounds by making columns of air vibrate. The longer the air column, the lower the frequency (pitch) of the note; the shorter the air column, the higher the sound's frequency or pitch.

You may have noticed the large hollow pipes in church pipe organs. The very low pitched notes come from the longer pipes; the higher notes come from the much shorter pipes. Although these organs are much larger than traditional woodwind instruments, the principle involved in making musical notes is the same—the vibration of air in a column.

A HOSE HORN

1. **Find a piece of garden** or shower hose at least 1 ft (30 cm) long. One end of the hose should have a screw-on connector to attach the hose to a faucet. Be sure the connector is clean. It can serve as the mouthpiece for your horn. Insert a plastic or metal funnel into the other end of the hose.

2. Put your lips against the mouthpiece and press them tightly together. Blow hard to produce the sound of a bugle. If you do not succeed the first time, don't be discouraged. With a little patience and practice, you may be able to play reveille for your family every morning.

   How can you change the pitch of the sound made by your horn? Hint: Make your lips vibrate as if you were blowing a raspberry. Then change the way you make your lips vibrate. How does this change the pitch?

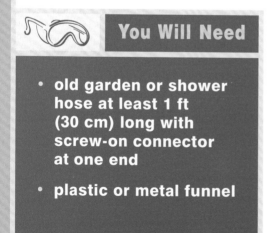

You Will Need

- **old garden or shower hose at least 1 ft (30 cm) long with screw-on connector at one end**

- **plastic or metal funnel**

3. Do you think the length of the hose has any effect on the sounds the horn makes when you blow into it? To find out, make a horn with a longer or shorter length of hose. What did you find?

A SIMPLE PIPE ORGAN

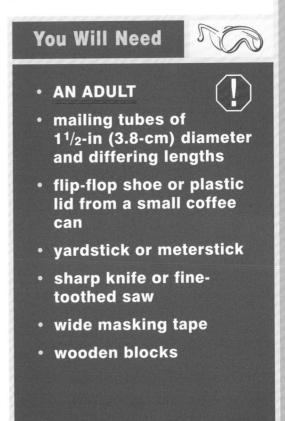

If you have ever listened to a pipe organ in a church, you know the instrument can produce sounds that have very low and very high frequencies. The long pipes are responsible for the low-pitched sounds, and the shorter pipes are the source of the higher-pitched notes.

1. To see how the length of the pipe affects the sound, find two mailing tubes with the same diameter that differ in length. Hold one of the tubes upright with your hand. Strike the top of the tube with a flip-flop shoe or a plastic lid from a small coffee can. Then do the same with the other tube. Which tube produces the higher pitched sound?

2. You can make a simple pipe organ from mailing tubes. Tubes with a diameter of 1 1/2 in (3.8 cm) work well. **Ask an adult** to help you cut or saw mailing tubes

You Will Need

- **AN ADULT**
- **mailing tubes of 1 1/2-in (3.8-cm) diameter and differing lengths**
- **flip-flop shoe or plastic lid from a small coffee can**
- **yardstick or meterstick**
- **sharp knife or fine-toothed saw**
- **wide masking tape**
- **wooden blocks**

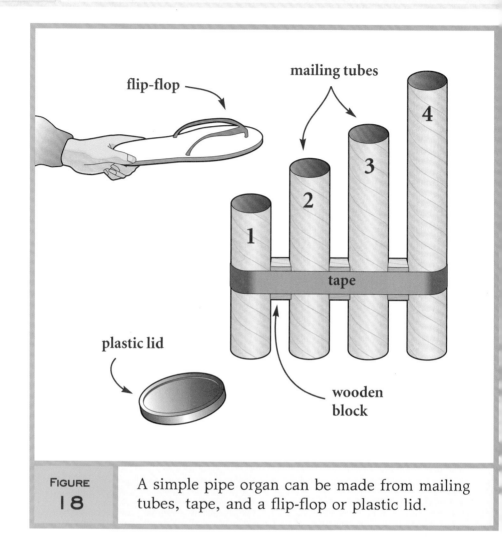

FIGURE
18
A simple pipe organ can be made from mailing tubes, tape, and a flip-flop or plastic lid.

that have the following lengths: 18 1/8 in (46 cm), 16 in (40.6 cm), 14 3/8 in (36.5 cm), and 11 3/8 in (28.9 cm). Leave both ends of the tubes open.

3. Lay the tubes side by side on a strip of wide masking tape. Place wooden blocks between the tubes. Then tape the tubes

together as shown in Figure 18. Label the tubes with the numbers 1, 2, 3, and 4, as shown.

4. Play a simple tune with your pipe organ. Hold the tubes upright. Use a flip-flop or a plastic coffee can cover to strike the tops of the tubes in the following order:

2, 3, 4, 3, 2, 2, 2, 3, 3, 3, 2, 1, 1

Do you recognize the tune as the first part of "Mary Had a Little Lamb"?

Can you play the rest of the song? Can you play other songs on your pipe organ?

A FLUTY HORN

1. **Ask an adult** to use a sharp knife to cut an $8\frac{1}{4}$-in (21-cm) length of plastic tubing that has an inside diameter of $\frac{5}{8}$ in (1.6 cm). Insert a mouthpiece from a party horn into one end of the tube. Then insert an 8-in– (21-cm–) long wood dowel of about the same diameter into the tube to make it rigid. Use a vise to hold the tubing and dowel in place.

2. **Ask the adult** to drill a $\frac{1}{4}$-in (6-mm) hole $1\frac{3}{4}$ in (4.5 cm) from the end of the tube that holds the mouthpiece. The adult may find it easier to start the hole with a hot nail. The sharp end of the nail can be heated by holding the nail, using pliers, in a flame. The adult can then drill five more

You Will Need

- **AN ADULT**
- **sharp knife**
- **plastic tubing with inside diameter of $\frac{5}{8}$ in (1.5 cm)**
- **ruler**
- **mouthpiece from a party horn**
- **wood dowel of about the same diameter and the same length as the inside of the plastic tubing**
- **vise**
- **drill and bit**
- **nail**
- **source of a flame, such as a gas stove**
- **pliers**

holes, 1, 2, 3, 4, and 5 inches farther from the end of the tube than the original hole. Again, it may be easier to start the holes with a hot nail.

3. Remove the dowel. Then blow into the flute with all the holes that were drilled uncovered. Listen to the pitch of the sound you hear. Now cover all six holes with your fingers. Do you think the pitch will be lower, higher, or the same when you again blow into the flute? Try it! Did you predict correctly?

    How does covering one or more holes with your fingers affect the pitch of the sounds when you blow into the flute? Can you play simple tunes on the fluty horn?

A BOTTLE BAND

1. **Find a clean, empty,** 1-L plastic bottle and a clean, empty, $\frac{1}{2}$-L (500 mL) plastic bottle. Blow across the mouths of both bottles. Blowing across the bottles will make the air in the bottles vibrate. Which bottle produces the sound with the lower pitch?

2. Fill one of the bottles halfway with water. Then blow across the bottle. Is the pitch of the sound you hear lower or higher than the pitch you heard when you blew across the empty bottle? Add more water to the bottle. Do you think this will increase or decrease the pitch you will hear when you blow into the bottle? Try it! Were you right?

3. Collect eight of these bottles. Fill them to different heights with water. Adjust the water levels in the bottles so that you can produce a full scale—*do, re, mi, fa, so, la, ti, do*[1]—when you blow across them. Label each bottle with the name of the note it makes.

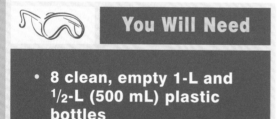

You Will Need

- **8 clean, empty 1-L and $\frac{1}{2}$-L (500 mL) plastic bottles**

- **water**

- **labels**

- **markers**

- **4 friends**

4. It is difficult for one person to play tunes with these bottles because it takes time to shift from one bottle to another. However, if you assigned two bottles each to four friends, your quartet could probably play simple tunes under your direction as conductor.

A PANPIPE

The panpipe is an ancient wind instrument consisting of tubes of different lengths. Each tube is sealed at one end. It is a wind instrument that you can play by yourself—no need for a band. Blowing across the open ends of the tubes of the panpipe produces sounds of different pitches. Panpipes are often made from bamboo. You can make one from $1/2$-inch (1-cm) plastic tubing or from a length of old garden hose.

1. If you have caps that will fit and seal the tubes, you can **ask an adult** to cut tubes with the lengths shown in Table 2. The tubes can be cut with a sharp knife or a hacksaw. The adult may need to smooth the ends of the tubes with a sharp knife.

2. If you do not have caps that fit the tubing, have the adult cut the tubes about $1/4$ in (0.5 cm)

longer. Then seal one end of each tube with modeling clay. Measure the desired length on an unsharpened pencil or dowel. Insert the pencil or dowel into the tube and gently tamp around on the modeling clay until the tube has the desired length given in Table 2.

TABLE 2	Lengths of the tubes needed to make a panpipe	
Length of tube in		**Note you should hear**
inches	**centimeters**	
5 7/8	15.0	*do*
5 1/4	13.4	*re*
4 3/4	12.1	*mi*
4 7/16	11.3	*fa*
3 15/16	10.0	*so*
3 1/2	8.9	*la*
3 1/8	7.9	*ti*
2 15/16	7.5	*do*[1]

3. Lay the tubes in order of length on a piece of masking tape as shown in Figure 19. Put a lump of modeling clay between the tubes to separate them by about 1/4 in (0.5 cm). Next, place a strip of masking or duct tape on and around the tubes to hold them together, side by side.

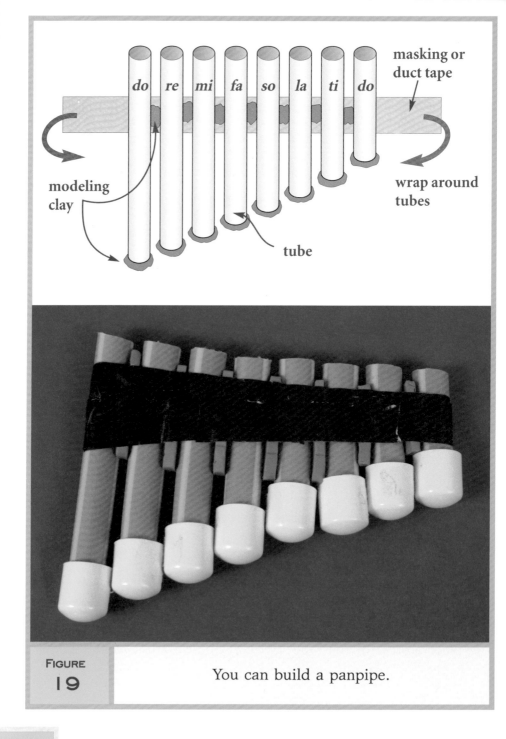

4. Which pipe do you think will produce the highest pitch (frequency) when you blow across it? Which pipe do you think will produce the lowest pitch (frequency) when you blow across it? Blow across each tube. Were your predictions correct?

Can you play a full scale on the pipes? Can you play some simple tunes?

IDEA FOR YOUR SCIENCE FAIR

Make a panpipe from soda bottles filled with water to different levels. Can you do the same with large test tubes?

REED HORNS

S ome woodwinds, such as the oboe, bassoon, saxophone, and clarinet, are reed instruments. Each has one or two flexible strips of metal or cane that fit into the instrument's mouthpiece. When air is blown across a reed, it vibrates. You can make a simple reed from a long, wide blade of grass.

1. Hold the blade of grass tightly between the sides of your thumbs. Put your mouth against your thumbs and blow hard over the blade of grass. The grass will vibrate and produce a squawking sound.

2. You can make a better reed from a drinking straw. Put one end of the straw into your mouth and flatten it with your teeth. Use scissors to cut that flat end of the straw so that it comes to a point (see Figure 20a).

3. Put the pointed end of the straw into your mouth. Press down on

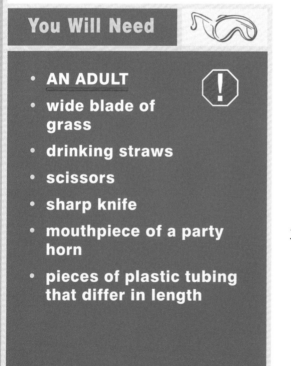

You Will Need

- **AN ADULT**
- **wide blade of grass**
- **drinking straws**
- **scissors**
- **sharp knife**
- **mouthpiece of a party horn**
- **pieces of plastic tubing that differ in length**

a)

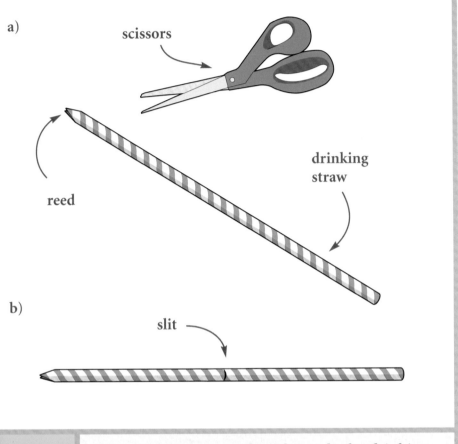

scissors

reed

drinking straw

b)

slit

	FIGURE 20	a) You can make a reed at the end of a drinking straw. b) **Have an adult** make a slit across the top of the middle of the straw so that you can bend the straw.

the straw with your lips just beyond the beginning of the pointed part. Then blow into the straw. You may need to experiment a bit to find the best position for your lips. When you find that position, you will hear a very distinct sound.

4. Do you think cutting the straw to make it shorter will affect the sound it makes? If you do, how do you predict it will affect the sound? Try it! Did you predict correctly?

5. Prepare another reed from a drinking straw. **Ask an adult** to use a sharp knife to make a slit halfway across the middle of the straw as shown on Figure 20b. What happens when you bend the straw while blowing a note? Can you explain why this happens?

6. Prepare a number of reeds from drinking straws. Then cut the straws into different lengths. Can you play a full scale of notes by choosing straws of different lengths?

7. You might ask your friends, each with a different-length straw, to form a reed band. With you as conductor, your band might play some simple tunes.

8. Remove the mouthpiece of a party horn from the rest of the horn. Look inside the mouthpiece. You will see a flap, or plastic reed. It vibrates when you blow into the mouthpiece.

9. Insert the mouthpiece into a piece of plastic tubing. When you blow into the mouthpiece, you will hear a sound. Do this with a number of plastic tubes that differ in length.

How does the length of the tube affect the pitch of the sound you hear when you blow into the mouthpiece?

IDEA FOR YOUR SCIENCE FAIR

From what you have learned about reeds, see if you can build a simple oboe that will play different notes.

PERCUSSION INSTRUMENTS

Percussion instruments are played by striking one solid object with another. A drum is played by striking a stretched membrane with a stick. The struck membrane vibrates, producing sound. Cymbals consist of two thin metal disks with handles attached to their centers. They are played by being brought together forcefully. The vibration of the edges of the cymbals results in a clanging sound.

If you dropped a number of sticks onto the floor at the same time, you would probably say they made a noise. But suppose you dropped a number of sticks of increasing length onto the floor one after the other. You would notice that the pitch of the sounds made by the sticks decreased with each stick that fell. Some percussion instruments, such as the xylophone and marimba, can be tuned. The xylophone consists of a number of wooden or metal bars of different lengths that are supported near their ends. When struck with a mallet, the bars vibrate and produce sounds with pitches characteristic of musical notes. The marimba is similar to the xylophone, but it has hollow tubes under the bars. Each tube is cut so that its length contains an air column. The tubes will resonate to the frequency of the bar that lies above it.

The marimba originated in Malaysia, spread to Bantu tribes in Africa, and then to Latin America. It is a very popular instrument with Latin American bands.

A Mechanic's Xylophone

1. **Place an empty cardboard egg carton** on a table or counter. Open the carton and lay steel wrenches of different lengths across the carton.

2. Using a metal spoon, gently tap each wrench. Which wrench produces the highest-pitched sound? Which wrench produces the lowest-pitched sound? How does the length of the wrench affect the pitch of the sound it emits?

   Can you play a simple tune by gently striking the wrenches with the spoon?

IDEA FOR YOUR SCIENCE FAIR

Examine a real xylophone, or a toy xylophone at a toy store. Notice how the metal or wooden slabs differ in length and are free to vibrate in place when struck with a small mallet. Then design and build a xylophone of your own using materials that you can find in your home or purchase at a hardware store. Once you have built your xylophone, see if you can modify it to make a marimba.

You Will Need

- **empty cardboard egg carton**
- **table or counter**
- **set of steel wrenches**
- **metal spoon**

DRINKING GLASS BELLS

A t banquets, the master of ceremonies often taps a water glass with a spoon to get the group's attention. The pleasant, high-pitched sound can be heard over the voices of a crowd. If the glass that is struck is nearly full, the pitch of its sound will be lower than if it is nearly empty.

1. Find a dozen or more tall drinking glasses or test tubes in a stand. You may need glasses of different sizes from more than one set to play a full scale. Sometimes the pitch difference between a full and an empty glass is less than an octave. Keep in mind the thickness of the glass as well as the amount of water it contains. Both are factors in determining the pitch of the sound it emits when struck lightly with a spoon.

2. Set the glasses or test tubes in a row. Nearly fill the first one with water and the next ones with progressively less water. You will find that they produce sounds of different pitches when struck lightly with a spoon.

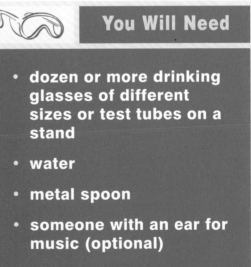

You Will Need

- **dozen or more drinking glasses of different sizes or test tubes on a stand**

- **water**

- **metal spoon**

- **someone with an ear for music (optional)**

Tune the glasses to play a full scale—*do, re, mi, fa, so, la, ti, do*[1]—by adding or removing water from the glasses. If you do not have an ear for music, ask someone who does to help you tune the glasses.

3. Once you have glasses that will play a full scale, play these notes:

do	*do*	*so*	*so*	*la*	*la*	*so*
fa	*fa*	*mi*	*mi*	*re*	*re*	*do*
so	*so*	*fa*	*fa*	*mi*	*mi*	*re*
so	*so*	*fa*	*fa*	*mi*	*mi*	*re*
do	*do*	*so*	*so*	*la*	*la*	*so*
fa	*fa*	*mi*	*mi*	*re*	*re*	*do*

Do you recognize the tune?

IDEA FOR YOUR SCIENCE FAIR

Bell choruses can often be heard during the holiday season. Examine the bells from such a chorus and see if you can explain how the bells are able to produce notes with different frequencies.

1. **Find two identical empty glass bottles** with narrow necks. Fill one about one quarter of the way with water. Fill the other about three fourths of the way with water.

   Which bottle do you predict will produce a higher pitch when struck lightly with a spoon? Try it! Did you predict correctly?

2. If you blow air across the mouth of the two bottles, which bottle do you predict will produce the higher pitch? (Hint: See Experiment 2-5.) Try it! Were you right?

   Blowing across the bottles reverses the high– and low-pitch frequencies you find when you tap the bottles with a spoon. Can you explain why?

   Can you, with friends to help you, combine tapping and blowing to produce tunes that everyone recognizes?

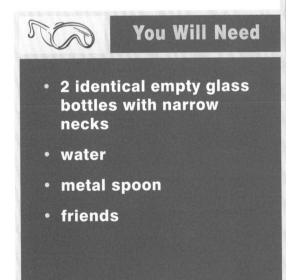

You Will Need

- **2 identical empty glass bottles with narrow necks**
- **water**
- **metal spoon**
- **friends**

A MECHANIC'S CHIMES

Many people like to hear chimes when a gentle wind causes them to strike one another. You can make a set of chimes, possibly from the same wrenches you used in Experiment 5-1. The wrenches should be of different lengths. At least one end of each wrench should have closed openings that fit over nuts or bolts. Such wrenches are called box-end wrenches.

1. Use a large nail to punch as many equally spaced holes as you have wrenches just inside the circumference of a rigid plastic lid. Punch one single hole in the center of the lid.

2. Use heavy string to suspend the wrenches from the holes around the lid. Thick knots at the ends of the strings should keep the strings from slipping through the lid.

You Will Need

- **set of steel wrenches that have closed openings on at least one end (box-end wrenches)**
- **large nail**
- **rigid plastic lid**
- **heavy string**
- **metal spoon**
- **tree limb**
- **hook, such as one used to hang a bird feeder**

3. A string through the center hole can be used to suspend the chimes from a tree limb or a hook, such as one used to hang a bird feeder. A second string through the center hole can be used to hang a metal spoon between the wrenches.

   When the wind blows, the spoon will strike the wrenches, which will also strike one another. Listen for ringing sounds when the wind blows.

BELLS FROM FLOWERPOTS

Clay flowerpots suspended from strings produce musical tones when struck by a wooden spoon. Generally, the larger the pot, the lower the pitch of the sound it makes when struck. However, because of differences in thickness and materials, pots of the same size may differ significantly in pitch.

1. Find a large collection of clay flowerpots on which you can play a full scale—*do, re, mi, fa, so, la, ti, do*[1]. Take with you a string attached to a small stick or a large paper clip. Slip the free end of the string through the hole in the bottom of a pot. Hold the string from which a pot is suspended with one hand. Strike the pot with a wooden spoon using your other hand. If you have a good ear for music, you can probably select eight appropriate pots. If you

You Will Need

- **8 clay flowerpots of different sizes**
- **string**
- **large wooden spoon**
- **small sticks or large paper clips**
- **someone with an ear for music (optional)**
- **long support such as a wire-grill shelf or long piece of dowel**
- **2 chairs or hooks**

lack such ability (and many people do), take someone with this ability along to help you select the pots.

2. Use string and small sticks or large paper clips to hang the pots from a long support such as a wire-grill shelf or a long piece of dowel supported by two chairs or hooks. Use a large wooden mixing spoon to gently strike the pots. Be careful not to hit the pots too hard. Even a slight crack will destroy the pot's characteristic tone.

WOOD CHIMES AND OTHER CHIMES

Wood strips of various lengths make different sounds when struck gently with a wooden dowel or wooden spoon.

1. Under adult supervision, make a set of chimes on which you can play simple tunes. To play a full scale, cut the lengths shown in Table 3 from 1-in × 2-in (2.5-cm × 5-cm) pine stripping.

2. Insert a screw eye in one end of each piece of wood. Suspend the wood strips from a support using string. Lightly strike each suspended strip, in turn, with a wooden spoon or a piece of wooden dowel.

You Will Need

- **AN ADULT** ⚠
- **20 ft (6 m) of 1-in × 2-in (2.5-cm × 5-cm) pine stripping**
- **8 screw eyes**
- **support such as a length of dowel, broom handle, curtain rod, etc.**
- **saw**
- **wooden spoon or wooden dowel**
- **sandpaper**
- **aluminum tubes, scraps of metal, metal forks and spoons, nails, pieces of bamboo, wood dowels, pieces of wood, or other items that can strike together in the wind**
- **rigid circular plastic lid**

TABLE 3	Lengths of 1-in (2.5-cm) × 2-in (5-cm) wooden chimes needed to play a full scale		
Length			**Note you should hear**
inches	**centimeters**		
20	50.8		*do*
19	48.3		*re*
18	45.7		*mi*
17 1/2	44.5		*fa*
16 1/2	41.9		*so*
15 1/2	39.4		*la*
14 1/2	36.8		*ti*
13 3/4	34.9		*do*¹

3. You will probably have to fine-tune the strips to play a full scale. The longer strips, as you have seen, produce a lower pitch. To raise the pitch, shorten the length of the strip. To do this, **ask an adult** to saw off or sand away part of the strip. If the pitch of a strip needs to be lowered, **have the adult** make a shallow saw cut across the middle of the strip. In either case, a little cutting can change the pitch significantly, so don't overdo it.

4. Once you can play a full scale, see if you can use your wood chimes to play simple tunes.

5. If you hang the strips from the circumference of a rigid plastic lid (see Experiment 5-4), you will have a set of wood chimes that can be hung outdoors. When the wind blows, you will hear gentle tones when wood strikes wood.

6. You can make wind chimes from a variety of materials. You might try scraps of metal, aluminum tubes, metal forks and spoons, various nails, pieces of bamboo, wood dowels, or other things you might think of. Suspend the items from a triangle-shaped frame made by nailing three pieces of wood together, or from a rigid circular plastic cover. The suspended articles should move freely in the wind so that they collide and make pleasant sounds. Hanging one piece in the center of the others will produce more notes.

IDEA FOR YOUR SCIENCE FAIR

The wooden strips have nodes (places that do not vibrate). If you suspend the wooden strips from their nodes, they can be hung horizontally, one below the other, on a single piece of twine. See if you can locate the nodes and arrange the wooden strips in this manner.

SAND BLOCKS

You can make an inexpensive percussion instrument from wood blocks and sandpaper.

1. Obtain two pine wood blocks about 1 ¹/₂ in × 4 in × 5 in (3.8 cm × 10 cm × 12.5 cm).

2. Buy a pair of cheap knobs at a hardware store. Using the screws that come with the knobs, attach the knobs to the center of each pine block's 4-in × 5-in surface.

You Will Need

- **AN ADULT** ⚠
- **two pine wood blocks about 1 ¹/₂ in × 4 in × 5 in (3.8 cm × 10 cm × 12.5 cm)**
- **drawer knobs**
- **screws**
- **screwdriver**
- **scissors**
- **different grades (grit numbers) of sandpaper or emery paper**
- **thumbtacks**
- **wood block**

- **dozen or more metal bottle caps**
- **hammer**
- **large nail**
- **smaller nails with a wide head**
- **cardboard or plastic picnic plates**
- **dried rice, beans, small bells**
- **stapler**
- **teaspoon**
- **2 8-oz plastic bottles with caps**

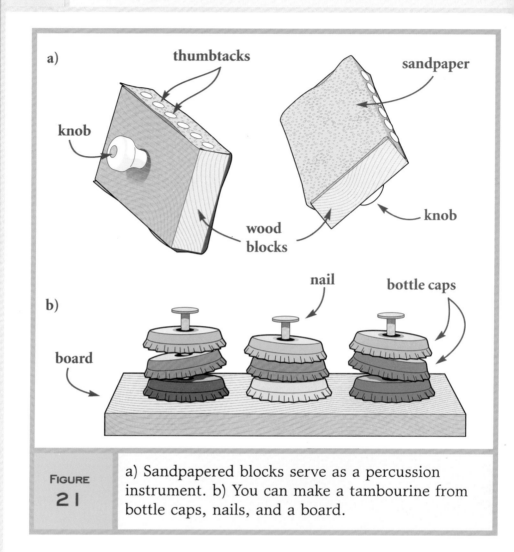

a) Sandpapered blocks serve as a percussion instrument. b) You can make a tambourine from bottle caps, nails, and a board.

FIGURE 21

3. Cut two pieces of sandpaper or emery paper to cover three sides of each of the two pine blocks, as shown in Figure 21a. Use thumbtacks to hold the sandpaper in place.

   When you rub the sandpaper surfaces together, you will hear a distinct sound.

4. Replace the sandpaper or emery paper with different grades of sandpaper or emery paper. Does changing the grade (grit number) of the paper change the sound produced when you rub the rough surfaces together?

TAMBOURINES

The tambourine is a common percussion instrument. You can make a very inexpensive one from bottle caps, nails, and a board.

1. Obtain a dozen or more metal bottle caps. **Ask an adult** to use a hammer and a large nail to make a hole in the center of each bottle cap.

2. Attach two or three bottle caps to a nail that has a wide head. Be sure the holes in the caps are wide enough so that the caps slide easily along the nails but do not slip over the head. Drive the nails partway into a wood block, as shown in Figure 21b.

3. Another tambourine can be made by placing some dried rice, beans, or small bells on a cardboard or plastic picnic plate. Cover with a second plate. Then staple the plates together.

4. Shake the board or plates and you will hear the sound characteristic of a tambourine.

MARACAS

Many bands have someone who creates a rhythm by shaking maracas. A maraca is a hollow gourd that contains beans or pebbles.

1. You can make a pair of maracas by pouring two or three tea-spoons of dried beans or rice into each of two 8-oz plastic bottles.

2. Cap the bottles and shake them.

Can you design and make maracas from other materials?

IDEA FOR YOUR SCIENCE FAIR

Find a large coffee can (33–39 oz) and a small one (11–14 oz). Both should have tight-fitting plastic lids. Use two pieces of thin wooden dowel or two pencils to beat the drums. How do the sounds produced by the two drums compare? Can you play a rhythm to accompany a tune on a radio or CD?

Arbor Scientific
P.O. Box 2750
Ann Arbor, MI 48106-2750
(800) 367-6695
http://www.arborsci.com

Carolina Biological Supply Co.
2700 York Road
Burlington, NC 27215-3398
(800) 334-5551
http://www.carolina.com

Connecticut Valley Biological
Supply Co., Inc.
82 Valley Road, Box 326
Southampton, MA 01073
(800) 628-7748
http://www.ctvalleybio.com/

Delta Education
P.O. Box 3000
80 Northwest Blvd.
Nashua, NH 03061-3000
(800) 258-1302
http://www.delta-education.com

Edmund Scientific
60 Pearce Avenue
Tonawanda, NY 14150-6711
(800) 728-6999
http://www.scientificsonline.com

Educational Innovations, Inc.
   362 Main Avenue
   Norwalk, CT 06851
   (888) 912-7474
   http://www.teachersource.com

Fisher Science Education
   4500 Turnberry Drive
   Hanover Park, IL 60133
   (800) 955-1177
   http://new.fishersci.com

Frey Scientific
   P.O. Box 8101
   100 Paragon Parkway
   Mansfield, OH 44903
   (800) 225-3739
   http://www.freyscientific.com

Nasco-Fort Atkinson
   P.O. Box 901
   901 Janesville Avenue
   Fort Atkinson, WI 53538-0901
   (800) 558-9595
   http://www.enasco.com

Nasco-Modesto
   P.O. Box 3837
   4825 Stoddard Road
   Modesto, CA 95352-3837
   (800) 558-9595
   http://www.enasco.com/science

Sargent-Welch/VWR Scientific
> P.O. Box 4130
> Buffalo, NY 14217
> (800) 727-4368
> **http://www.SargentWelch.com**

Science Kit & Boreal Laboratories
> 777 East Park Drive
> P.O. Box 5003
> Tonawanda, NY 14150
> (800) 828-7777
> **http://www.sciencekit.com**

Wards Natural Science
> P.O. Box 92912
> 5100 West Henrietta Road
> Rochester, NY 14692-9012
> (800) 962-2660
> **http://www.wardsci.com**

Ardley, Neil. *Music.* New York: Dorling Kindersley Publishing, Inc., 2004.

Bardhan-Quallen, Sudipta. *Championship Science Fair Projects: 100 Sure-To-Win Experiments.* New York: Sterling, 2004.

Bochinski, Julianne Blair. *More Award-Winning Science Fair Projects.* Hoboken, N.J.: John Wiley and Sons, 2004.

Dispezio, Michael A. *Super Sensational Science Fair Projects.* New York: Sterling Publishers, 2002.

Dunleavy, Deborah. *The Kids Can Press Jumbo Book of Music.* Tonawanda, N.Y.: Kids Can Press Ltd., 2001.

Levine, Shar, and Leslie Johnstone. *Science Experiments with Sound & Music.* New York: Sterling Publishing Co., Inc., 2002.

Parker, Steve. *The Science of Sound: Projects and Experiments with Music and Sound Waves.* Chicago: Heinemann, 2005.

Rhadigan, Joe, and Rain Newcomb. *Prize-Winning Science Fair Projects for Curious Kids.* New York: Lark Books, 2004.

The Physics Classroom: Sound Waves and Music
http://www.physicsclassroom.com/class/sound/soundtoc.html

Making Sounds with Musical Instruments
http://www.school-for-champions.com/science/sound_music.htm

INDEX

A

African thumb piano, 67–68
antinodes, 42, 43

B

banjos, 60, 73–77
basses, 60, 81–84
bells
    drinking glass, 107–108
    flowerpot, 112–113
bell/woodwind mystery experiment, 109
bicycle experiment, 22–23
bottle band experiment, 94–95
bottle experiment, 25
box/pot experiment, 18–19
brass instruments. *See also* specific instruments.
    overview, 87
    vibrating air column experiment, 51–53
bridges, in stringed instruments, 60, 62–63, 70, 74, 75–76
bugles, 88
bull roarer experiment, 21

C

candle flame experiment, 29
cardboard/paper resonance experiment, 55–56
cellos, 60
chimes, 110–111, 114–116
compression, 27, 28
concordant, 45
cymbals, 104

D

discordant, 45
drums, 104
dyads, 47

E

eight-string harp experiment, 78–80

F

flowerpot bells, 112–113
flutes, 87, 92–93
frequency. *See also* pitch.
    defined, 14
    fundamental, 43–44
    natural, 54–55, 59
    octaves and, 36, 45–47
    ratio and, 45
frequency, in experiments
    balloon, 17
    bicycle, 22–23
    string, 39, 40

G

gases, sound waves in, 32, 50, 59
guitars
    one-string, 69–72
    overview, 60, 61
    shoe box, 85–86

H

harmonics, 43–44
harps, 61, 78–80
hearing ranges, 17, 20
Hertz, Heinrich Rudolf, 14
hertz (Hz) defined, 15
hollow part, stringed instruments, 60, 64
hose horn experiment, 88

I

infrasound, 20

K

kazoos, 18

L

liquids, sound waves in, 32–35, 57–58, 94–95

longitudinal waves, 27–28, 29

M

mailing tube experiments
    pipe organ, 89–91
    resonance, 57–58, 59
mandolins, 60
maracas, 120
marble experiment, 25
marimbas, 104–105, 106
megaphone experiment, 31
Middle C, 23, 45–47
musical notes, vibrations and, 14
music overview, 7–8
mutes, on stringed instruments, 62–63

N

nodes, in sound waves, 42–43

O

octaves, 36, 45–47, 72
one-string guitar experiment, 69–72
organs, 87, 89–91
overtones, 44

P

panpipe experiment, 96–99
people-pushing experiment, 25–26
percussion instruments
    bells, drinking glass, 107–108
    bells, flowerpot, 112–113
    bell/woodwind mystery
      experiment, 109
    chimes, 110–111, 114–116
    maracas, 120
    overview, 104–105
    sand blocks, 117–119
    tambourines, 119–120
pianos
    harmonics experiment, 45–47
    strings, 54, 55, 57, 61
    twangy experiment, 67–68
    wide-key experiment, 65–66
Ping-Pong ball/tuning fork
    experiment, 19
pipe organs, 87, 89–91
pitch. *See also* frequency.
    defined, 16
    octaves and, 36, 45
    in percussion instruments,
      107–116
    resonance and, 54–59
    in stringed instruments, 60,
      67–72, 81–86
    in woodwinds, 51–53, 87,
      89–99
pitch, in experiments
    balloon, 17
    bells, flowerpot, 112–113
    bell/woodwind mystery, 109
    bicycle, 22–23
    bottle band, 94–95
    chimes, 110–111, 114–116
    drinking glass bells, 107–108
    flutes, 92–93
    hose horn, 88
    one-string guitar, 69–72
    panpipe, 96–99
    pipe organs, 87, 89–91
    ruler, 16–17
    shoe box guitar, 85–86
    string, 37–40
    twangy piano, 67–68
    vibrating air column, 51–53, 57
    washtub bass, 81–84
    waxed paper, 18
    wineglass, 18
playground swings, 54–55
Pythagoras, 36, 45

R

rarefaction, 28
ratio and frequency, 45–47
reed instruments, 100–103
resonance, 54–58, 59
rope experiment, 41–44

S
safety issues
    rules overview, 12–13
    warnings, 8–9
salt grain experiment, 18–19
sand blocks, 117–119
science fairs
    overview, 9–11
    report formats, 12
scientific method, 11–12
Slinky experiment, 26–28
solids, sound waves in, 32–35, 48–50
sonar, 20
sound
    human ear, detection of, 17, 20
    overview, 14
    ultrasound/infrasound, 20
    vibrations, 14, 15–19
sound box, stringed instruments, 60, 64
sound trumpet experiment, 31
sound waves
    antinodes, 42, 43
    nodes, 42–43
    overview, 24–30
    rope experiment, 41–44
    in solids/liquids/gases, 32–35, 48–50, 57–58, 59, 94–95
standing waves, 41–44
stringed instruments
    bridges, 60, 62–63, 70, 74, 75–76
    hollow part, 60, 64
    mutes on, 62–63
    overview, 60–61
    pitch in, 60, 67–72, 81–86
string experiment, 37–40
string telephone experiment, 48–50

T
tambourines, 119–120
tetrads, 47

transverse waves, 27–29
triads, 47
two-string bottle banjo experiment, 73–77

U
ultrasound, 20

V
vase/tube experiment, 57–58
vibrating air column experiments, 51–53, 57
vibrations, 14–19, 21. *See also* pitch.
violins, 60, 64

W
washtub bass experiment, 81–84
watch experiment, 32–34
water wave experiment, 29–30
wavelength, 42, 43
wind instruments, 87. *See also* woodwind instruments.
woodwind instruments. *See also* brass instruments; reed instruments.
    bottle band experiment, 94–95
    flute experiment, 92–93
    overview, 87
    panpipe experiment, 96–99
    pipe organ experiment, 87, 89–91
    pitch in, 51–53, 87, 89–99
    vibrating air column experiments, 51–53, 57

X
xylophones, 104–105, 106